SEP 2017

CO-SLEEPING

Parents, Children, and Musical Beds

Susan D. Stewart

ROWMAN & LITTLEFIELD
Lanham • Boulder • New York • London

Published by Rowman & Littlefield
A wholly owned subsidiary of
The Rowman & Littlefield Publishing Group, Inc.
4501 Forbes Boulevard, Suite 200, Lanham, Maryland 20706
https://rowman.com

Unit A, Whitacre Mews, 26-34 Stannary Street, London SE11 4AB,
United Kingdom

British Library Cataloguing in Publication Information Available

Library of Congress Cataloging-in-Publication Data Available
ISBN 978-1-4422-4905-9 (cloth : alk. paper)
ISBN 978-1-4422-4906-6 (electronic)

♾ ™ The paper used in this publication meets the minimum requirements of
American National Standard for Information Sciences Permanence of Paper
for Printed Library Materials, ANSI/NISO Z39.48-1992.

Printed in the United States of America

For Gwen

CONTENTS

ACKNOWLEDGMENTS

I would like to thank my husband, daughter, and family for their support during what turned out to be a four-year project. I also appreciate the support of Iowa State University for granting me a faculty professional development assignment that provided me with the time to conduct this research and write this book. I thank the Midwest Sociological Society's Research Grants Program for funding this research and my former PhD student and research assistant, Dr. Adrienne Riegle, for her work conducting interviews and contributing to conference presentations. I also thank my colleagues and conference participants for their valuable feedback. I am incredibly grateful to Rowman & Littlefield for their support and especially Sarah Stanton for seeing the value of this project. Lastly, I want to extend my sincere appreciation to the parents, and their children, who participated in the study, warmly welcomed me into their homes, and shared with me some of the most intimate aspects of their lives, and without whom this project would not have been possible.

1

CO-SLEEPING IN THE UNITED STATES

Why Are We So Different?

Parents and children sleeping together is referred to as *co-sleeping* or, should they occupy the same bed, *bedsharing*. In 2011, a segment on the *Today Show* reported the results of a Columbia University study of 944 toddlers who regularly slept in the same bed as their mothers.[1] The study found no negative effects of co-sleeping on the intellectual or social development of these children, which the researchers assessed at several points in time up through the age of five. The study was newsworthy for two reasons. First, the American Academy of Pediatrics (AAP) recommends against bedsharing with children during infancy because of its association with sudden infant death syndrome or SIDS and many pediatricians discourage co-sleeping with children of any age.[2] Second, co-sleeping is not widely practiced in the United States and is generally disapproved of by Americans. Parents who co-sleep with their children are commonly thought of as new-age hippie types. They're those long-skirted moms who make their own baby food and breastfeed their school-aged children; they're those babywearing, sandal-clad dads at the farmer's market.

The initial *Today Show* story was followed up with another that focused on a public service advertisement created by the

Milwaukee Health Department. In the ad, which was placed on billboards around the city, an infant is shown cuddled-up with a butcher knife. The tagline read, "Your baby sleeping with you can be just as dangerous." Whereas the news of the first study did not create much of a splash, the second produced an immediate negative reaction and a flurry of activity on social media. Not surprisingly, a third set of stories soon followed: "Bed-Sharing with a Toddler: Should Moms Feel Guilty?," "Coming Out of the Bed-Sharing Closet," and "Go Ahead, Let Your Kids Climb into Bed with Mom and Dad."

These stories and others like it create a quandary for parents. Engage in a practice that feels to some parents natural and good, and risk your children with what would seem like certain death. Prioritize your children's safety, and suffer through sleepless nights of letting them "cry it out."[3] New parents unwittingly find themselves in the middle of a highly charged debate and are surprised to learn that how and where their children sleep is "an issue." According to *Parents Magazine*, co-sleeping is among the top ten parenting debates facing modern parents.[4]

Expectations for parents have never been higher. Some commentators have even referred to modern parenting as a new "religion" that is "killing the American marriage."[5] Parents, in their quest to make the "right" decisions for their children, feel compelled to sift through piles of information on infant care, an overwhelming and confusing process. In a recent study of the results of Google searches on "infant sleep position" and "infant sleep surface" and eleven related terms, more than half of the websites provided inaccurate or irrelevant information (in relation to American Academy of Pediatrics recommendations).[6] Well-meaning relatives and friends often feel the need to weigh in on the subject as well. In the end, as I discovered in the process of doing the research for *Co-Sleeping: Parents, Children, and Musical Beds*, parents who co-sleep with their children often keep their sleeping arrangement to themselves or limit their conversations to a few trusted friends and family members.

Americans' ambivalence toward co-sleeping is interesting given that co-sleeping is practiced in the majority of countries around the world. Why then, in the United States, is co-sleeping so controversial? One possibility is America's reverence for medicine and our "medicalized" approach to what most consider routine life course events—most notably, birth and death, but increasingly, parenting. The Columbia study cited above, published in the prominent medical journal *Pediatrics*, was conducted by specialists in public health and medicine. And as noted above, the medical community has historically taken a negative view of co-sleeping. Two years later, a study of co-sleeping conducted by researchers at the Yale School of Medicine was published in the *Journal of the American Medical Association*.[7] Whereas the Columbia study focused on the effect of co-sleeping on children's well-being, the Yale study focused on its associated demographic factors. Even so, the researchers referred to co-sleeping as an "unhealthy trend" with "strong links to sudden infant death syndrome."[8] An article in *Psychology Today* referred to the modest rise in co-sleeping as "disturbing news."[9] Proponents of co-sleeping point out that the health benefits of co-sleeping far outweigh the risks, and that culture rather than science underlies Americans' low rates of co-sleeping.[10] Nevertheless, a sizable percentage of Americans consider co-sleeping unsafe and only a minority of U.S. parents sleeps with their children.[11]

IS CO-SLEEPING SAFE?

In the United States and other places around the world, infant mortality steadily declined throughout the twentieth century. After a brief plateau between 2000 and 2005, the U.S. infant mortality rate declined another 12 percent between 2005 and

2011 and is now at an all-time low of six infant deaths per one thousand live births.[12] Nevertheless, the United States has higher infant mortality than the vast majority of industrialized nations, ranking twenty-sixth in a list of twenty-nine European countries, ranking behind Japan, Korea, Israel, Australia, and New Zealand.[13] Researchers attribute this difference to higher economic inequality in the United States and specifically to its greater number of premature births as a result of higher rates of smoking, substance use, poverty, and lack of prenatal care among lower income groups.

In 2013, 3,434 U.S. infants died "suddenly and unexpectedly." This category of death, referred to as sudden unexpected infant deaths (SUID), was created by the National Center for Health Statistics to capture infants whose cause of death was not immediately obvious prior to investigation. In 2013, sudden infant death syndrome (SIDS) accounted for 45 percent of SUID deaths. The remainder was attributed to "unknown causes" (31 percent) and "accidental suffocation and strangulation in bed" (24 percent).[14] Cause-of-death data analyzed by the National Center for Health Statistics showed a steady decline in SUIDs in the last two decades, and in 2016 they were at their lowest level in history.[15] Even so, worries about SIDS weigh heavily on the minds of parents and are, as I found in my research, the major reason why they hesitated to co-sleep.

Numerous studies have found that co-sleeping, specifically bedsharing, is a risk factor in infant death. However, sudden infant death syndrome is not well understood and the relationship between co-sleeping and SIDS is hotly debated, even among researchers. For example, a number of studies indicate that co-sleeping is dangerous to infants only in the presence of other risk factors, such as when the adults in the home smoke, are overweight, or use drugs. Other risk factors include young maternal age, not receiving adequate prenatal care, not breastfeeding, overbundling, and placing the child prone or belly down to sleep.[16] In most documented cases of SIDS, multiple risk factors were present.[17] Proponents of co-sleeping argue that under most conditions co-sleeping is very safe, if not advantageous. For example, the rate of SIDS is lowest in Asians countries where co-sleeping is the norm.[18] Moreover, SIDS deaths have declined during a time of rising rates of co-sleeping.

Attitudes about co-sleeping are evolving, however. For example, The American Academy of Pediatrics recently updated their recommendations for what is considered a safe sleeping environment for infants. These new guidelines finally "acknowledge the reality" that despite the warnings, many babies sleep in their parents' bed, either unintentionally (for example if the mother falls asleep breastfeeding) or by choice. Their recommendations continue to emphasize putting infants to sleep on their back; providing a firm sleep surface free of blankets, pillows, and stuffed animals; breastfeeding; avoidance of exposure to smoke, alcohol, and illicit drugs; and parents' not putting their baby in bed with them. What is new is that they now recommend that infants sleep "in their parent's room, close to their parents' bed, but on a separate surface designed for infants."[19]

It is being increasingly recognized that co-sleeping can have both positive and negative effects on parents and children. First are the potential negative consequences. Based on data from a national poll conducted by the National Sleep Foundation (2004), researchers found that, compared to children who slept alone in their own bed, children who shared a bed with someone else were more resistant to going to bed, got fewer hours of sleep, had more frequent nighttime waking, had greater difficulty falling asleep, and were more likely to be identified by their parents as having sleep problems.[20] In a sample of preschoolers, bedsharing was associated with significantly lower scores on child temperament, more frequent night-waking, greater intensity of emotion to parental disapproval, lower ability to be coaxed away from forbidden activities, and less consistent eating habits.[21] Co-sleeping may not necessarily be responsible for sleep disruptions in families however. Rather, sleep disruptions may encourage families to co-sleep. A number of parents I interviewed for this book co-slept in response to their children's sleep problems.

How does co-sleeping affect parents? Again, the research is mixed. In a study of Israeli families, co-sleeping was associated with lower parental satisfaction among both mothers and fathers and disrupted sleep among new mothers.[22] Consistent with the belief that co-sleeping disrupts the marital relationship, one study found a negative relationship between co-sleeping and marital satisfaction although this effect was observed only among couples who did not intend to co-sleep.[23] The relationship between co-sleeping and negative outcomes may not hold in some cultures, however. For example, whereas co-sleeping was associated with bedtime struggles, night-waking, and sleep problems among U.S. families, these effects were largely absent in Japanese families where co-sleeping is common.[24] On the other hand, another study found more sleep problems among Chinese children than American children.[25]

In spite of these studies of the short-term effects of co-sleeping, researchers have been unable to establish that co-sleeping has serious, long-term negative effects on children's physical and psychosocial development.[26] In addition to the research mentioned above, a Dutch study found co-sleeping in infancy was not associated with anxiety or depression in children at age three.[27]

Other research has found co-sleeping to be associated with numerous health benefits. Co-sleeping is associated with higher rates of breastfeeding as well as regulation of breathing and a reduction in the stress hormone cortisol, at least in the short term. The latter effects have been observed for both parents and children.[28] Other research suggests that not soothing a crying baby, whether at night or during the day, can have long-term consequences for these children in adulthood, such as a diminished capacity to handle stress and higher levels of anxiety, insomnia, attachment disorders, and even chemical dependency.[29] Co-sleeping may accelerate the development of the child's neurological system.[30] Moreover, in contrast to the widely held belief that co-sleeping creates abnormal attachments to caregivers, co-sleeping with one's parents as a child has been linked to positive personality traits, confidence, and independence in adulthood.[31]

Some research indicates that co-sleeping is good for parents. Although not directly measuring the effect of co-sleeping, one study found that mothers who did not comfort their crying child after placing them down for their nighttime sleep (i.e., letting them "cry it out") experienced increased cortisol levels.[32] Until this book, there were no studies of fathers and co-sleeping. Some research suggests that co-sleeping may be beneficial to children and fathers.[33] For example, children whose fathers work at night have more disrupted sleep; children's sleep is sensitive to changes in their parents' work schedules.[34] In another example, co-sleeping fathers were found to have lower testosterone levels than other fathers, which could translate into an improvement in fathering.[35] Others have found greater activity in areas of the brain associated with parent-child synchrony and nurturance among fathers who spent more time in the direct care of their infant child.[36]

Overall, the health effects of co-sleeping are probably dependent on a host of factors and any differences in children who co-sleep compared to those who do not is probably small. For example, parental presence at sleep onset (holding or rocking the baby to sleep) has been shown to have a stronger positive effect on children's sleep behavior than did co-sleeping.[37] Moreover, regardless of where children sleep, having a consistent bedtime routine has been found to be the most consistent predictor of sleep quality of children.[38] Clearly, co-sleeping is a complex phenomenon needing further exploration.

GOALS OF THE BOOK

Co-Sleeping: Parents, Children, and Musical Beds is neither an indictment nor endorsement of co-sleeping. My aim in this qualitative study is not to make claims about whether co-sleeping is good or bad. This book is also not intended to be used as a tool for parents making the decision to co-sleep, although the information presented in the study may help in this process. It is also not a guide on how to sleep safely with your children, as there are numerous books specifically on the subject, such as *Three in a Bed*, by Deborah Jackson and *Sleeping with Your Baby*, by James McKenna.[39] However, this book serves several purposes. One is descriptive. One of my initial goals was to document the sleeping arrangements and nighttime routines of contemporary American families. Given our increasing understanding of the importance of sleep to our overall well-being, this is an important subject, but there has been little research on sleep in families. Thus, one of the main goals of the study was to discover *how* co-sleeping families actually sleep.

Co-Sleeping also delves into *why* co-sleeping families sleep as they do—also an understudied topic. Therefore, a second objective of the book was to provide insight into parents' motivations, perspectives, and feelings about co-sleeping. Previous research on co-sleeping has been heavily focused on its consequences for children, but there are consequences for parents as well. Yet, very little is known about parents who co-sleep in terms of their day-to-day lives, hopes, fears, and how co-sleeping fits into their broader beliefs about parenting.

A third goal of the study was to gain additional insight into the implications of co-sleeping for relationship dynamics. Although it is well-known that couples' relationship quality declines after the birth of a child and stays low until children leave the nest, the reason for this are not fully understood. In *Co-Sleeping* parents provide rich descriptions of how co-sleeping affects their relationships with their spouses and partners. Finally, co-sleeping must be studied in relation to the current cultural and social environment. Thus, the book describes how parents handle co-sleeping with respect to their pediatrician, friends, family members, and a largely disapproving public.

WHY I WROTE THIS BOOK

I am a sociologist specializing in the study of families. My ongoing research agenda focuses on how family dynamics affect child and adult well-being. Truthfully, however, my own personal experience with co-sleeping probably provided the greatest motivation to study the topic. My daughter did not sleep with my husband and me as a baby or toddler. We, too, had an intense fear of SIDS to the extent that I never put my daughter on my chest or even held her if there was any chance I might fall asleep. Things changed, however, after my husband and I divorced when my child was three-and-a-half. Soon after, she started coming to my door and asking to sleep with me. She didn't ask me every night, and she didn't sleep with me necessarily the whole night, but we slept together pretty regularly. Although her desire to sleep in my bed has waned considerably (she is thirteen), she still sometimes asks to sleep with me and I sometimes let her. Today, this includes sleeping not only with me, but with my new husband. I wondered (and still do): Is this weird? Is this wrong? But letting my young daughter sleep with me felt right, and sometimes still does, even with these questions. It also turns out, all this time, my daughter had also been asking to sleep with her dad when she was with him at his house. While he wouldn't let her sleep in the bed, he allowed her to sleep in a sleeping bag on the floor of his room. He told me he still sometimes allows her to sleep with him if she's not feeling well or is having trouble sleeping.

Soon after the *Today Show* story aired in 2011, it seemed like co-sleeping was everywhere in the news. Mayim Bialik's (star of the 1980s sitcom *Blossom* and now of *The Big Bang Theory*) book *Beyond the Sling* came out and became a bestseller.[40] Bialik, who has a PhD in neuroscience, is a strong advocate of attachment parenting, a progressive parenting style developed by Dr. William and Martha Sears, of which co-sleeping is an integral part. Numerous other news stories soon followed in *Redbook*, *The Washington Post*, *Scientific American*, and *The Atlantic*, to name a few. These articles for the most part came to the conclusion that co-sleeping is not harmful, and may even be helpful, but in general, is "not a big deal." Interestingly, another stream of articles emerged about the same time, one of which appeared in the *New York Times*. These focused not on parents and children sleeping together, but on parents themselves sleeping *apart*.[41]

I have many friends with school-aged children. It turns out that quite a few of them have or are currently co-sleeping with their children. As was the case for me, their choices did not fit our society's common understandings of co-sleeping. The practice of co-sleeping is not necessarily everyone piling into the "family bed" at night; nor is it something only practiced by new parents or Sears followers. Rather, it appeared, at least from my informal discussions with fellow parents, that co-sleeping involves a diverse group of parents, children of different ages, and a variety of sleeping arrangements. Among my fellow parents, co-sleeping served a variety of purposes, both philosophical and practical, and those parents experienced a range of feelings about it. Many did not define what they were doing as "co-sleeping" per se and did not label it as such. My initial conversations with friends were anecdotal and did not constitute research. However, when I conducted the interviews for this book, I found support for all of these themes and more.

After the Columbia study came out finding no long-term negative impacts of co-sleeping on children, I did a quick search in Google Scholar to find out if there were any studies of co-sleeping by sociologists or other social scientists as opposed to pediatricians and other medical researchers. There were not many. Those that did exist mostly focused on families in countries other than the United States. A more general Google search resulted in mostly scary stories of the dangers of co-sleeping and advice books for parents on how to get their children to sleep in their own bed. Given this rather surprising gap in knowledge, my hope is that my book will be useful in providing basic information about how families with children sleep, how parents interpret their family's sleeping arrangements, and how these arrangements impact parents' relationships both inside and outside the home.

NATIONAL TRENDS IN CO-SLEEPING

It is difficult to estimate the number of parents and children who co-sleep. Studies define co-sleeping differently, the age of the children varies from study to study, and many parents are reluctant to report they co-sleep. However, studies provide a picture of the overall trends. For example, available studies agree that most American parents and children do not co-sleep.[42] According to the National Sleep Foundation's *2014 Sleep in America Poll*, only about 8 percent of children sleep in the same bed with someone else.[43] However, several different data sources indicate that co-sleeping is on the rise.[44] The American Academy of Pediatrics' *National Infant Sleep Position Study* found that the number of parents sharing a bed with an infant increased from 6.5 percent in 1993 to 13.5 percent in 2010.[45] As expected, co-sleeping is more common among families with younger children. About 12 percent of infants, 8 percent of toddlers, 11 percent of preschoolers, and 4 percent of school-aged children sleep in their parents' bed "most of the night.[46] A longitudinal study found that co-sleeping increased from 10 percent in infancy to 38 percent at age four (presumably because older children can get out of bed on their own), and then declined thereafter, suggesting that co-sleeping is a "transient" phenomenon rather than a permanent pattern.[47] The reason for the rise is unclear, but, as I explain later, the rise in co-sleeping may be linked to increases in women's employment, progressive parenting styles, increased media attention and information on the Internet, and the busy, time-compressed lifestyles of modern families. And as I mentioned earlier, co-sleeping is one of the three main prongs of attachment parenting. This parenting style is being adopted by a growing number of U.S. parents.[48] Co-sleeping may also be connected to the rise in single motherhood that has occurred over the last few decades.[49] Nevertheless, although there was a brief increase in public awareness of co-sleeping in the 1970s with the publication of Tine Thevenin's *The Family Bed*, the practice remains largely outside mainstream parenting.[50]

UNIQUE FEATURES OF THIS BOOK

Few published studies of co-sleeping have been conducted by social scientists and almost none have been conducted by sociologists. Since sleeping and its routines and rituals are an integral part of family life, this is surprising. Moreover, most research is not accessible to a general audience and is usually in the form of scientific journal articles and books designed for academics. Although this book will appeal to academic readers, it is also intended for parents and others interested in the topic. I've found that the books available on the topic do not take a balanced approach to co-sleeping, with most resources (including websites, blogs, and other forms of social media) focusing on the dangers of co-sleeping and the difficulties that co-sleeping creates. Or, they take a decidedly positive view, having been written by and for staunch supporters of this practice. As opposed to fueling further debate, my intention with *Co-Sleeping* is to provide a balanced, scientific view of co-sleeping for all the aforementioned audiences.

One of the book's unique features is that it focuses on co-sleeping families in the United States. Similar studies have been based on families from Japan, Israel, and other countries.[51] While valuable, these sources are limited because family life in the United States is culturally distinct, often referred to as "American Exceptionalism." In particular, families in the United States tend to have more conservative values, norms, practices, and attitudes about social and moral issues. Some distinctive features of American family life are higher fertility and marriage rates, more traditional parenting styles (such as higher rates of corporal punishment—i.e., spanking), greater religiosity, and a medicalized approach to childbirth.[52] Because of these lifestyle differences, international studies cannot provide much insight for understanding co-sleeping among American families.

Second, because previous research on co-sleeping focuses almost exclusively on co-sleeping with infants and toddlers, very little is known about co-sleeping with older children. For *Co-Sleeping: Parents, Children, and Musical Beds*, I interviewed parents who currently co-slept with children ages twelve and under (although some parents also had older children that were included in the conversation). My study addresses many other limitations of available research. Both mothers and fathers were interviewed. Men have generally not been studied by co-sleeping researchers except in relation to their breastfeeding wives.[53] This is problematic given recent increases in father involvement, which is associated with better cognitive, emotional, and behavioral outcomes in children.[54]

Finally, the participants interviewed for *Co-Sleeping* are, to my knowledge, more diverse than in any other study of co-sleeping. Parents were actively recruited from different racial/ethnic groups, different family forms (single, cohabiting, [re]married), and different income levels. Participants were of various sexual identities (heterosexual, gay, lesbian). My sample included parents from a diverse array of educational backgrounds, occupations, and income levels. Examining how such factors affect sleep patterns is becoming increasingly important as the U.S. population continues to diversify; co-sleeping may have different effects depending upon one's membership in these groups.[55] For example, studies have found higher levels of co-sleeping among single mothers.[56] These diverse voices will be interwoven throughout each chapter.

EVOLUTIONARY, HISTORICAL, AND CROSS-CULTURAL PERSPECTIVES

One of the main goals of this book is to document and describe the nighttime routines of modern families, an understudied yet important context for understanding family intimacy, relationship dynamics, and child and adult well-being in U.S. families. Most American parents are juggling work and family roles and are experiencing a high level of stress.[57] According to the Bureau of Labor Statistics, in 60 percent of married-couple families with children, both spouses work.[58] In her book *Longing and Belonging: Parents, Children, and Consumer Culture*, Allison Pugh makes the point that the expense of raising a child will continue to increase as what is considered childrens' "basic needs" continue to expand.[59] The individualistic and competitive culture of the United States, combined with poor institutional supports for families, such as paid parental leave and subsidized childcare, may compound the pressures on modern parents. Moreover, our understanding of what constitutes a "good" parent is changing. Coinciding with women's mass entry into the workforce, sociologist Sharon Hayes put a name to the trend, *intensive mothering*.[60] Intensive mothering involves substantial supervision of children, a high level of involvement in children's academics and activities, and continuous monitoring of their achievement. It is rigid and rule oriented, competitive, and individualistic. Parents are expected to take sole responsibility for their children's success, and failures.[61] This way of parenting is quite different from parenting in Europe and Latin America, where parents are much more "laissez-faire."[62] This shift has been extended to fathers as well. Now referred to as *intensive parenting*, this parenting style, for better or worse, is now the prevailing model of parenting in the United States.

Given the shift in parenting expectations and changes in women's roles, it is not surprising that families are finding it increasingly difficult to get enough sleep. Societal awareness of the importance of sleep has been increasing for some time. The Centers for Disease Control and Prevention calls insufficient sleep a "public health epidemic," and report that 35 percent of adults get less than seven hours of sleep a night.[63] New mothers and fathers average about six hours a night and their sleep is often disrupted.[64] Data from the National Sleep Foundation indicate that Americans' sleep hours and quality has declined significantly since 2001. For example, 64 percent of Americans reported a sleep problem at least a few nights a week, up from 51 percent in 2001.[65] Children of all ages routinely get less sleep than their parents think they need; 10 percent of parents rated their children's sleep as "fair" or "poor."[66] Epidemiological studies indicate that sleep disorders in children are being underdiagnosed.[67] Poor sleep has been shown to be associated with a host of negative outcomes for adults and children including anxiety, reduced work productivity, aggression, obesity, poor school performance, lower marital happiness, and increased mortality.[68] Two recent books delve into the "science of sleep": David Randall's *Dreamland* and Kat Duff's *The Secret Life of Sleep*.[69] Numerous studies have shown that adopting good sleep habits is one of the most effective ways to preserve one's physical and psychological health.

Sleep is a result of complex interactions between biology, culture, and interpersonal dynamics. Generally, sleep is viewed as a solitary activity, but it is a social phenomenon as well, and should be examined in the context of the family.[70] Seventy-eight percent of adults sleep in the same bed with someone else,[71] and numerous studies have shown that individual family members' sleep patterns affect one another's health and well-being.[72] *Two in a Bed* by Paul Rosenblatt, provides an excellent description of myriad factors affecting one's (and one's partner's) sleep, including temperature, snoring, bathroom trips, nightmares, teeth grinding, as well as basic tossing and turning.[73]

Evolutionary theory would suggest that co-sleeping promotes close family bonds and feelings of security. Because sleeping requires "a relative cessation of awareness and responsiveness to the external environment," it is thought that sleeping together provided early humans with social cohesion, security, and protection from external threats.[74] It makes sense that letting infants "cry it out" would attract predators.[75]

Although sleep is a biological necessity, important cultural differences, with respect to when, how, and with whom we sleep, exist. As noted above, co-sleeping remains widespread in other cultures and occurs in most African, Asian, and Central and South American countries. According to data from the *2013 International Bedroom Poll*, the percentage of adults who reported sleeping with children on most nights ranges from 9 percent in Germany, 10 percent in the United States, 11 percent in the United

Kingdom, 14 percent in Canada, 17 percent in Mexico, and 33 percent in Japan.[76] In a study of 3,700 infants in Thailand, 68 percent shared a bed with their parents and another 32 percent shared the same room.[77] Co-sleeping is also prevalent in Scandinavia and Southern Europe.[78]

In non-Western countries, sleep is fluid, occurring at various points during the day or night, and under many different conditions, such as during boisterous family celebrations.[79] In more traditional societies, children and adults sleep in close proximity and children often do not have set bedtimes and are allowed to stay up late.[80] In contrast, Americans engage in prolonged and uninterrupted periods of solitary sleep. Rather than falling asleep naturally, children go to sleep at set times and stay asleep in their beds. Over the last fifty years, American children are increasingly expected to follow strict sleep schedules to accommodate work, school, and extracurricular activities. In the *2014 Sleep in America Poll* conducted by the National Sleep Foundation, more than 80 percent of American parents reported having a regular bedtime for their children on school days, that is "always" or "usually/ sometimes" enforced.[81] That study found that more than two-thirds of parents with children under the age of fifteen had six or more sleep-related rules, such as no electronics or caffeine in the evening. The use of "transitional objects" such as special blankets and teddy bears are common in American families, and are thought to substitute for human contact. Self-soothing behaviors such as thumb sucking are also more prevalent in cultures in which families do not co-sleep.[82] In the United States, children's ability to go to sleep on their own, and stay asleep, is considered a developmental milestone.[83]

Children's sleeping alone is a relatively recent pattern associated with industrialization and modernization. It occurs most commonly in individualistic, as opposed to collectivist, cultures and reflects American values of independence and self-reliance.[84]

Children and parents' each having their own rooms was seen as a sign of achieving middle-class status.[85] In the United States, co-sleeping is more prevalent among racial and ethnic minorities.[86] In the United States, Asians and Hispanics (28 percent and 22 percent) have the highest rates of co-sleeping, followed by African Americans (15 percent) and Whites (8 percent).[87] In general, co-sleeping is also more prevalent among economically disadvantaged populations.[88]

That co-sleeping is currently more common among lower socioeconomic groups is consistent with historical data on the practice. In preindustrial America, co-sleeping was widely practiced. However, co-sleeping declined with industrialization and growth of the middle class, especially after World War II. Parenting guru and author Dr. Spock, widely read during the middle part of the twentieth century and considered the "father of modern parenting" encouraged flexibility, affection, and play, but disapproved of co-sleeping. It was thought that children must "learn" how to sleep on their own, and parents engage in a variety of rituals to facilitate this, such as bath time and reading stories.[89]

Sharing beds and bedding was common in Europe in the preindustrial period, and among the poor this practice continued into the modern era. In the book, *At Day's Close: Night in Times Past*, historian A. Roger Ekirch describes how family members (and overnight guests) routinely slept three or four or more to a bed or shared bedding on the floor. Co-sleeping was not considered a bad thing. Aside from mealtimes, few opportunities existed for families to gather together, and sleeping together provided "a critical source of domestic cohesion."[90] Family members' sleeping places were often determined by gender and age, sisters next to mothers and sons next to fathers, with the men nearest the door to fend off intruders. Farm animals were also routinely brought in at night. Even among the middle and upper classes, having a "bedfellow" was considered a good thing, providing warmth, security, and companionship.[91]

In his research, Ekirch found that before the Industrial Revolution, nighttime was something to be feared. For example, evidence from the premodern period suggests that young children have an innate fear of the dark. Parents therefore sometimes created "night games" for their children to feel more comfortable, increasing their exposure to the dark incrementally. This theme is echoed in Craig Koslofsky's book, *Evening's Empire: A History of Night in Early Modern Europe*. He explains that in the absence of modern technology, darkness "imposed fundamental limits on daily life."[92]

Koslofsky notes that as societies modernize, they undergo a process of "nocturnalization," in which human activity gradually expands into previously unutilized nighttime hours. For example, by the end of the fifteenth century, all over Europe coffeehouses stayed open late into the night. These places were reserved for men, however. The vast majority of women, aside from the urban elite who attended concerts and cultural events, remained largely in the private sphere, and some coffeehouses banned women. In general, women who appeared in public after dark were assumed to be of "questionable virtue."

Importantly, it would be a mistake to assume that *nothing* happened during the night back then. Whereas formal institutional activities have historically tended to halt at nightfall, more private, family activities never have. In medieval and early modern Europe, the night was segmented into two parts, "first sleep" and "second sleep," with a range of activities occurring in short intervals between, such as prayer, conversation, sex, and tending to children.[93] Anthropologists have found evidence of segmented sleep in societies that do not use artificial light.[94] In preindustrial Europe, work often began before dawn and continued into the night by candlelight. Although working at night was generally discouraged, industries such as farming, brewing, and forging continued into the nighttime hours. Of course, wives and domestic servants worked around the clock. Tasks such as knitting, spinning, and sewing requiring less light were frequently conducted at night by firelight and it was not uncommon for friends and neighbors to stay overnight.[95]

Despite this history, our current knowledge of modern family life has been, for the most part, restricted to daytime hours. As a result, we know very little about the organization of families' nighttime hours and routines. That we are currently living in a "24/7 economy" is well-known. Activities previously only taking place during the day now often take place during the night for a large segment of the population (nowadays fueled by Starbucks). More than half (54 percent) of employed Americans work *nonstandard hours*, or work more than half their hours outside of 8 a.m. to 5 p.m. or on weekends.[96] Therefore, sleeping, though primarily a nighttime activity, for many people occurs during the day. These changing work roles have consequences for parenting and family life. For example, in 60 percent of dual-income married couples with children under age five, at least one spouse works nonstandard hours and/or weekends, and 25 percent of dual-income couples work "split shifts" (i.e., spouses work opposite hours).[97] Because daycare is often financially out of reach for families, and because daycare is hard to find outside standard work hours, many husbands and wives share childcare responsibilities through a system of "tag team" parenting. In these families, parents may see each other briefly in the morning or at night between shifts.

These trends have important consequences for sleep quality, especially for women. For example, sociologist David Maume and his colleagues studied the sleep patterns of married couples in which one spouse worked nights.[98] Their findings indicated that wives' sleep was more often disrupted than husbands' and seeing to the needs of children explained a large part of the difference in wives' abilities to get continuous sleep. Other studies found similar results with respect to gender differences in the amount and quality of sleep, with women, especially single mothers, experiencing worse sleep than do men.[99]

THEORETICAL APPROACH OF THE BOOK

The theoretical approach of the book is based on Andrew Weigert's concept of the "sociology of everyday life."[100] This refers to the importance of studying the ordinary, day-to-day aspects of human existence that provide texture and meaning to what are generally considered more central life events. Despite its importance, the "everyday" has largely been ignored by researchers. Sociologist Kerry Daly refers to these forgotten features as "negative spaces," which he defines as "recessive areas that we are unaccustomed to seeing but that are every bit as important for the representation of the reality at hand."[101] According to Daly, an important negative space is "the location of family members in time and space."[102] This would include the organization of the family home, which, especially in modern American families, is largely hidden from public view.

A second theoretical perspective utilized in this book is that of family stress, originated by Pauline Boss.[103] As noted above, modern American families are dealing with a range of stressors, including work-family balance, financial problems, relationship issues, and lack of leisure time. Such stressors are linked to poorer family outcomes.[104] *Co-Sleeping* explores the role co-sleeping plays in this mix of challenges. Finally, taking an ecological approach is vital for understanding sleep.[105] This approach views the family as a *system* of relationships operating not unlike a mobile hanging over a baby's crib—a touch to one spoke reverberates through the others. Family dynamics are complicated, and one family member's poor sleep can negatively affect the whole family.

HOW I STUDIED CO-SLEEPING IN FAMILIES

Co-Sleeping: Parents, Children, and Musical Beds is based on interviews with fifty-one parents from two medium-size, Midwestern cities. Parents self-identified as co-sleeping with their children. In the recruiting materials, *co-sleeping* was defined as one or both parents sometimes or regularly sleeping with their children (age twelve and under) in the same bed or room at night (or part of the night). The definition was kept purposely broad to capture the fullest possible range of families' sleeping arrangements. For example, parents and children did not necessarily have to sleep in the same bed (referred to as *bedsharing*) nor did they have to sleep together the whole night or every night. Previous studies typically measure co-sleeping as where the child "sleeps the majority of the time," which does not capture the full range of co-sleeping behaviors. [106]

I recruited my participants by posting flyers in places where parents tend to congregate (schools, health clubs, libraries, etc.), and by making announcements at parents' groups such as MOPS (Moms of Preschoolers). Other participants were recruited through "snowball sampling" using networks of parents connected to one another through their children's various academic, social, or sports activities. Recruitment materials were designed to capture both *intentional co-sleepers*, parents who endorse the ideology of co-sleeping, and *reactive co-sleepers*, parents who co-sleep in reaction to children's nighttime problems, such as nightmares. [107] Toward that end, my recruiting posters contained two photographs. The first showed a family sleeping peacefully together with smiles on their faces. The other showed a grumpy-looking family with disheveled sheets and the children lying crosswise on the bed.

Interviews began with the participant's filling out a brief demographic survey, consisting of questions such as gender, race/ethnicity, education, employment, income, as well as characteristics of his or her spouse or partner, if applicable. The number, ages, and genders of the children in the family were recorded. Participants then took part in an in-depth, semi-structured interview lasting approximately one hour. The interview was comprised of four modules: (1) logistics, (2) feelings, (3) relationships, and (4) secrecy/openness. These components are described in more detail later on.

I used what social scientists refer to as a "grounded theory" methodology in my analysis of the interviews, in which ideas, concepts, and themes are allowed to naturally emerge from the data.[108] I transcribed the interviews by hand and found Johnny Saldana's book, *The Coding Manual for Qualitative Researchers*, very useful in this process.[109] I relied upon Miles and Huberman's book *Qualitative Data Analysis* for verifying my results, drawing conclusions, and theory development.[110] Throughout my analysis, I practiced "reflexivity," in that my own subjective commitments, experiences, and feelings will be "acknowledged, confronted, and integrated" into the analysis.[111]

Co-Sleeping focuses on four specific aspects of co-sleeping. The first is *logistics*, which contains a description of a "typical night" of families who co-sleep, such as the location of all sleepers in relation to one another, the movements of sleepers during the night, and the surface on which sleepers sleep (bed, floor, couch, crib, etc.). The second is *feelings*, which includes parents' perspectives, such as their level of satisfaction and/or dissatisfaction with co-sleeping. The third is *relationships* and how co-sleeping affects parents' intimacy with their spouse/partner (including sexual intimacy), as well as with their children, relatives, and friends.

The fourth aspect of the study is *secrecy/openness*, which address-es parents' comfort level with discussing the family's sleeping ar-rangements and the possible reactions of others such as their pediatrician, family members, and friends.

CHARACTERISTICS OF PARTICIPANTS

Parents who co-sleep in the United States are often assumed to be highly educated, white, liberal-minded, attachment parenting followers. Although some parents in my study practiced attach-ment parenting (or otherwise practiced child-centered parent-ing), the participants in my study are demographically diverse and most were outside this group. On the one hand, this diversity was by design. I purposely sought out parents of different ages, races, genders, family types, education levels, occupations, religious in-volvement, and income levels. Nevertheless, the diversity of the sample reflects those parents who saw my advertisements around town and signed up for the study. I also posted an announcement about the study to an attachment parenting group on Facebook that yielded a number of inquiries, but in the end these parents made up less than one quarter of my sample.

In a written survey, participants provided basic demographic information on themselves (gender, age, race/ethnicity, educa-tion, income, etc.), their children (number, age, gender, etc.), and other information I thought would be relevant to the family's sleeping arrangements. These include the parents' occupations and work hours. For example, many parents worked split shifts and were the only parent at home with the children at night. Although most were married, I collected detailed information on parents' marital status. Finally, I collected information on relig-ious affiliation and church attendance, which I thought might be reflective of parents' values about family life and parenting. A table describing the demographic characteristics of the sample is located in the appendix.

The sample of 51 participants is comprised of 38 mothers and 13 fathers, and contains 11 couples (2 fathers were married but their wives did not participate). The participants were in their childbearing years but varied in age with 11 between 20 and 29 years old; 28, age 30–39; and 9 were age 40 and over (in 3 cases, information on age was not recorded). Forty-one participants were White, 2 were Black, 3 were Hispanic, 3 were Asian, and 2 were mixed race or some other race.

The parents in the study had a total of 101 children. Seventeen parents had one child, 23 had 2 children, and 11 had 3 or more. The gender of the children varied from 10 parents with all girls, 22 parents with all boys, and 19 parents with a mix of boys and girls. Twenty-nine parents had children age 2 or younger, 33 had preschool age children, 22 had children 6–8 years old, 9 had children age 9–12, and 8 parents had children age 13 and older. Although a criterion for participation was having a child 12 or under with whom they currently co-slept, it is important to note that parents with more than one child were not necessarily co-sleeping with all of them (although some were). However, most parents with multiple children reported having co-slept with their older children, too. Eighty-seven of the 101 children resided in the home full-time, 7 lived elsewhere (either on their own or with another parent), and 7 lived in the home part-time. Ninety-two of the children were the biological children of the parent, 7 children were adopted, and 2 were stepchildren.

Thirty-nine of the 51 participants were married. Of those who were unmarried, 6 were cohabiting (4 of whom were cohabiting with their child's biological father). The remaining 6 parents had a serious romantic partner, were dating, or were not currently dating. Seven parents reported having been divorced. Regarding education, 17 participants had at least some college, 12 had a four-year degree, and 20 had some graduate education or a graduate degree. Only 2 participants did not have training beyond high school.

The employment characteristics reflect that the sample is predominantly comprised of women. Of the 51 participants, 30 were employed part-time, 28 worked full-time, and 10 were stay-at-home parents. Thirty-eight said they had jobs with "some" or "a lot" of flexibility in their work hours; only 3 participants said they had "none." Of those who worked outside the home, 34 worked at least some non-standard hours (outside the hours of 8 to 5); only 7 did not. The participants were employed in a range of fields and professions. The mothers in the sample were teachers, nurses, counselors, childcare providers, in medical and health occupations, publishing, public relations, sales, and retail. The professions of the fathers included professors, graduate students, and research scientists (reflecting the college community within which many participants were drawn). However, I also interviewed a rifle instructor, mechanic, tow truck operator, freelance writer, mortgage analyst, IT specialist, shipping supervisor, delivery driver, and a collegiate umpire.

Regarding religion, about half of participants (25) reported no religious affiliation. The remainder was split between various religions. Four were Catholic, 7 were Protestant, 3 were Jewish, and 12 were of some other religion. Twenty-three parents said they did not attend church, 15 attended yearly, 8 attended monthly, and 5 attended weekly. The participants had a range of incomes. Fifteen reported a household income of less than $50,000, 15 had incomes between $50,000 and $74,999, 13 had incomes between $75,000 and $99,999, and 7 had incomes $100,000 or greater. One participant did not report their income.

PLAN OF THE BOOK

The book covers the logistics of co-sleeping (chapter 2), parents' feelings about co-sleeping (chapter 3), how co-sleeping affects parents' relationships (chapter 4), and parents' level of openness with respect to talking with others about the fact that they co-sleep (chapter 5). I described the interviewees in terms of whether they are a mother or a father, their marital status, their race, their number of children, as well as their gender, and ages. Chapter 6 provides a summary of overall findings, their implications, and a broader discussion of how co-sleeping fits into the lives of contemporary American parents. The limitations of the study are also discussed.

Hopefully, this book will provide parents with reassurance that there is no "right" way to parent, that having ambivalent feelings toward one's children is a normal part of parenting, and that co-sleeping may or may not fit into the equation. Academics, doctors, and parenting "professionals" can say what they want, but parents are the true experts on their children. They care for them, love them, and generally know what's best for them. Hopefully the stories presented here will reinforce this notion and provide comfort and support to families regardless of when, where, and how they sleep.

2

CO-SLEEPING LOGISTICS

Who, When, Where, and How Families Sleep

INTERVIEWER: The first thing I want to ask is about just logistics. What is a typical night like for you and your family?

ALLISON (married with three children ages twelve, nine, and six): Well, my older two children usually sleep by themselves. My son sleeps in his room, my older daughter sleeps not in her room, but in her sister's room, and my little one, she sleeps with us. She just goes to sleep in bed with us, and when my husband's not home, my middle daughter also sleeps with me and my younger daughter. My husband will just go to bed in whichever bed is the convenient bed to go in. We used to call it "musical beds." And now, it's pretty much how we sleep.

The first step toward understanding parents and children who co-sleep is to get an accurate picture of the specific patterns and activities that occur during families' sleep time. This chapter details the nighttime hours of co-sleeping families, including the location of all sleepers in relation to one another, movements of sleepers during the night, and the surface on which sleepers sleep (bed, couch, crib, etc.). These descriptions also include the origin of these patterns, any changes in patterns, and any attempts to change them.

As discussed in chapter 1, research on sleeping arrangements in families is sparse. Studies also do not provide much insight into variation in co-sleeping based on parents' gender, age, race/ethnicity, marital status, education, or employment, nor does it say much about how the number, gender composition, and ages of the children might affect co-sleeping patterns. The goal of this chapter is to describe the full diversity, fluidity, and complexity of co-sleeping in a wide range of American families. The information presented is based on the portion of the interview in which parents were asked to describe the sleeping activities and behaviors that occur on a "typical" night in their home. All names of parents, children, family members, and others have been changed to protect their confidentiality.

SLEEPING CONFIGURATIONS AND DYNAMICS

Returning to Allison:

> INTERVIEWER: When they sleep with you are they in between you two or are they on mommy's side?

> ALLISON: No, they're in the middle.

> INTERVIEWER: And is she a good sleeper?

> ALLISON: She does shove me out of bed. Like if I'm on the edge and she's right next to me and then there's my husband on his side and there's a *huge* space . . .

> INTERVIEWER: Do you or your husband ever get up and move to a different location?

ALLISON: He doesn't tend to. I will if I get too hot or if I am getting smushed out. I sometimes sleep on the couch and sometimes I go to sleep with my other daughter.

INTERVIEWER: Does she have a double bed?

ALLISON: Yeah, we have—our smallest bed is a double bed—we have big beds for that reason.

Allison and her husband have actively created a co-sleeping environment by having a king-sized bed for themselves and double beds for each of the children. The arrangement is not without its drawbacks, such as, as she explains, getting overheated or pushed out of the bed. It becomes apparent from this interview that it is not only children who are mobile during the night. Parents—in this case, Allison—may also move to another location during the night.

Recall from chapter 1 that that *bedsharing* refers specifically to parents and children who sleep together in the same bed. Co-sleeping can include bedsharing and usually does, but also includes a wider set of behaviors subsumed under "sleeping together." In this study, *co-sleeping* was defined as *one or both parents sometimes or regularly sleeping with their children in the same bed or room at night or part of the night.* I purposely kept this definition broad to capture the widest range of sleeping arrangements. For example, this definition was designed to detect co-sleeping dynamics, including both nighttime movements and changes in sleep patterns over time. For example, Allison's story demonstrates that both children and *parents* may change location during the night. It was also not uncommon for children and parents to make multiple moves over the course of a single night. Moreover, many families' sleeping arrangements varied from night-to-night and were different for different children in the same family. Their sleeping arrangements also evolved over time.

These changes depended on a host of factors including the children's ages, parents' work schedules, and the birth of siblings. Therefore, the distinction between bedsharing and co-sleeping proved to be quite important.

Bedsharing

Although parents reported a diversity of sleeping arrangements, most of the families were, at least in part, bedsharers. This was the case regardless of the children's age, race and ethnicity, gender, class, and the other demographic characteristics examined.

Families with Infants

Compared to families with toddlers and older children, families with infants were more likely to share their bed with their child, mainly because co-sleeping facilitates breastfeeding and according to most parents was "easier" and just "made sense." Co-sleeping was seen as a practical matter for parents who desired to feed their child on-demand or who did not want the hassle of constantly getting out of bed to feed their child. For most of the families I interviewed, the mother was responsible for feeding the child and breastfed exclusively; few fathers bottle-fed the child breast milk or formula. Most parents with infants said that co-sleeping allowed the mother to "get more sleep." Ingrid's second daughter started out in a "rock-and-play" and slept there for about four months. She said, "Then I started putting her in our bed because I nurse at night so whenever she would wake up, I would just kind of pull down my shirt and she would nurse and we would fall back asleep so then I never really had to wake up." Savannah and her husband slept with their ten-month-old daughter. They first tried having their child sleep in a crib in the next room but, "the difficulty was hearing her cry and not going in there to pick her up. She doesn't really stop crying unless you go in there and pick her up. So, it doesn't really seem to work. She was sick for most of the month of November and ever since then the only way we could get her back to sleep was to bring her to our bed and it just continued." Karen had a similar experience:

> I remember being just so tired of lifting him out of the co-sleeper to get him and put him next to me to nurse him. We hadn't mastered the whole sideline nursing thing. That took a while. I remember the next night. I was just too tired. I can't have him over there. He needs to be next to me. And I had been against it! I was like, "I don't want the kid in the bed with me. I'm afraid I'll roll over on them or something."

As Karen had, many of these parents did not intend to co-sleep but found it had many advantages.

When parents with infants shared the bed, the most common arrangement was having the baby sleep on the outside next to the mother. Less frequently the baby slept in-between his or her parents or switched sides throughout the night. Most parents were afraid to put the baby in the middle of the bed. Evelyn explained, "I kept him between the wall and me. I was scared of my fiancé rolling on him, so I just kept him next to me." There were no cases of infants sleeping on the father's side of the bed. My findings were similar to a home study conducted by Sally Baddock and her colleagues.[1] They used nighttime video surveillance to gather information on co-sleeping families in New Zealand. In their study all the infants slept beside their mothers, separated from fathers and other siblings. The fathers seldom had contact with their infant during the night, and slept facing away from the infant. Another home study, by Helen Ball, of co-sleeping families in the United Kingdom found that in more than two-thirds of the cases, the baby slept between his or her parents, with the remainder sleeping on the mother's side.[2] However, in families where the child slept in the middle, the mother slept facing the child and fathers slept facing away from the child. In that study, fathers exhibited less synchronicity with their child than did mothers. Whereas the mother nearly always awoke with their child's arousals, the majority of fathers slept through them.

Although I myself never brought up the topic of sudden infant death syndrome (SIDS) with the parents, all of them expressed the concern early in the interview that bedsharing would increase their baby's risk of SIDS. Some parents slept with their child anyway. However, a number of parents adopted a "modified" bedsharing style by using a co- or side-sleeper. Anthony and Samantha explained, "We used that Snuggle Nest for the first six or seven weeks because we were more comfortable with that. We talked about it quite a bit, and I was always paranoid that I was going to roll over on him." Samantha continues, "You're [speaking to her husband] a much heavier sleeper than I am so for him to sleep in between us you felt more comfortable in the Snuggle Nest. At about six or seven weeks we started bedsharing without the Snuggle Nest."

Parents could be quite creative in an effort to ensure their baby's safety. David and Renee have three boys. David explained, "For all of the children we had a crib set up right next to Renee's side of the bed that was level with our bed. It's a waterbed frame. It's a wooden frame that was hard so she would cover it with a blanket. But otherwise it was level so we kind of extended the bed in a sense with the crib." Renee continued,

> We took one side off and so it was completely closed. It had wheels but the wheels were locked. I also had something that went all the way under. Over the baby's mattress and underneath it and then it went inside our box and under our mattress. So, it was not like the baby was going to be trapped in the middle and, you know, be strangled.

Families with Toddlers and Older Children

As would be expected, toddlers and older children had more diverse sleeping configurations than families with infants, but most shared the bed with their parents (as opposed to just sleeping in their parents' room). Co-sleeping with older children was more disruptive to parents however. Many parents mentioned being "pushed," "grabbed," and "poked." Carley described what it was like to sleep with her six-year-old son: "He kicks and punches me in the middle of the night. He doesn't have a clue what he's doing. Last night he smacked me in the head. Conked my head! He's got a watermelon for a head and he smacks you with it." Allison (from the beginning of the chapter) eventually purchased large beds for everyone to accommodate her family's fluctuating sleep habits. Like Carley, her sleep was frequently disrupted. For example, she often moved as a result of being overheated and mentioned being pushed out of the bed from time to time. Other parents described sleeping on a little "sliver" of the bed and worried about themselves falling out.

Alternative Arrangements

Co-sleeping families did not always share the same bed. Alternative arrangements were moving the child's bed into the parents' room, parents and/or children sleeping on the floor, parents sleeping apart, and siblings sleeping together.

Rooming-In

A number of the children slept in their parents' room but not in their bed. Sometimes parents moved their children's crib or bed into their room. This was often pulled up next to the bed. Ingrid and Victor had their king-sized bed and their three-year-old daughter's twin bed pushed together in their room. Many couples did this with their child's crib. Amanda is married and has a nine-month-old daughter. She explained,

> At first we had the crib "sidecar-ed" on our bed. We took the front rail off and tied it to the bed essentially so it wouldn't scootch away. Then we took the crib out and we put a mattress on the floor next to our bed thinking I could lie on the mattress [with her] and get her to fall asleep and then get up and go into bed myself. Sometimes, frankly, I'm just tired and don't care if I'm sleeping on a mattress on the floor. And so I just end up sleeping there with her.

Sleeping on the Floor

Parents and children sleeping on the floor was not uncommon. For example, Janice is married and has a two-year-old son who she and her husband had difficulty keeping in his bed. She described her son's sleeping routine:

> JANICE: [Our son] will sometimes come into our bedroom. Maybe around three in the morning or something, he'll come in. He'll do either one of two things. He'll either come in and wake me up because of past issues. I then proceed to put him back in his bed and tell him it's still, you know, sleeping time. Or, he will curl up on the floor next to my bed and not tell me and he will go to sleep. If I don't hear him come in in the middle of the night, he'll sleep there until we wake up in the morning.

Because their child continued to come into their room at night and slept on the floor, they modified their plan to accommodate what some parents in the study called "bumps in the road." As with Brad and Mandy, the modification was less Janice and her husband's idea than their child's. Many parents in the study considered such arrangements (e.g., sleeping on the floor) at least progress toward their child's sleeping independently.

A number of parents reported themselves sleeping on the floor of the children's room or on the floor elsewhere in the house. For example, Scarlett was reluctant to co-sleep but still wanted to be close to her child. She said,

> [Our son] was in his own room in a crib. Maybe when he was a year old just putting him in the crib always woke him up. So we just put the crib mattress on the floor and we started lying next to him for him to go to sleep. After several months of that my husband said, "Why don't you just bring him into bed with us? He'll be happier. We'll be happier." And I was like, "No, no!" You know there's a social stigma against it. Kids are supposed to sleep in their own room! But I remember distinctly feeling that I just wanted to take a sleeping bag next to his crib and sleep there.

Becky also feared SIDS and her child's rolling out of bed and was reluctant to co-sleep. She said, "As an infant she would wake up usually every hour at night. I finally got to the point where I was just so exhausted so I would just lie on the floor. I just didn't feel comfortable putting her in bed with me. It just started out in desperation and just continued because I like sleep." Another parent, Matthew, spent a lot of time on the floor and sometimes slept there. He explained,

> There were lots of times actually that for our son I'd be bouncing him, laying on the living room floor, just trying to get him to go to sleep. Or I'd be holding him lying against the cabinet in the kitchen with my eyes closed. There were numerous other times where I would lie on the floor with my arm through the crib, you know, patting.

Parents Sleeping Apart

As was the case in Paul Rosenblatt's study of the sleep patterns of couples, many of the parents I interviewed slept separately.[3] Both Tammy and her husband, Gene, wanted their seven-year-old son to sleep in his own bed in his own room. Tammy explained that he would not go to sleep in his room unless one of them slept with him in his bed. However, their son still sometimes slept with them in their bed. When their son slept with them, especially if "he's thrashing about," Gene would go sleep on the couch. William Sears in his book, *Becoming a Father* (2003), described many examples of fathers sleeping on the couch or in another room.[4]

Returning to the parents in my study, Evelyn and her boyfriend have a one-year-old son together. She said,

> Well, my boyfriend and I live together. We sleep in separate rooms. The baby sleeps in the room with me in a rock-and-play, which is kind of like a bassinet but it rocks and it's at an incline and it's directly next to the bed within arms' reach of me. My boyfriend sleeps in what was originally going to be the guest room and is now kind of turned into his bedroom in essence. [*laughs*]

There were a number of instances in which the mother was the one to change location. When I asked Amy who was more likely to move, she responded, "He does occasionally but I'm more likely to move. He's a heavier sleeper and he has sleep apnea and snores. So sometimes it's an out for me when she comes over if he's being disruptive, too. I just leave the two of them to their own devices." This was also the case for Wendy:

> It isn't ideal, but he snores and she wakes up if there's noise. Most of the time he's in the guest room. But there were a lot of nights when [our daughter] likes to cuddle, which is sweet, but sometimes the cuddling involves feet in the back and if I'm just not getting any sleep we'll switch places so we both spend time co-sleeping with her. So he does spend a fair share in there, too.

Many mothers mentioned their husbands' snoring as one of the reasons they slept apart. Becky explained, "Each of my children have their own rooms and they always go to bed in their rooms. My son stays there all night. My daughter stays in her bed about half the night and then usually sneaks into bed with me. My husband usually falls asleep on the couch. He's a heavy snorer. He does that by choice because if he came to bed with me, then I'd be on the couch."

Siblings Sleeping Together

One surprise of the study was the number of children who slept together. Brad and Mandy have two children ages five (daughter) and three (son). As discussed in chapter 1, children's sleep disruptions are generally handled by mothers. Brad's intimate knowledge of his children's sleep patterns is therefore notable. Below, he provides a detailed description of the nighttime activities of his family, which involved the children, sleeping together.

> BRAD: We start bedtime with the kids generally around 7:30. It's a process for us. First, we have story time. Each child picks their own story. Either [Mandy] or I (we alternate back and forth) sits with the kids and reads the stories. Once the stories are over, they say good night to the parent that is not reading the stories. Then generally speaking we'll lie with the children in bed for, on average, about ten minutes. That sort of settles them down. We have music playing, night-lights, and all that good stuff. Generally speaking, by the time we leave the room they are either falling asleep or in some cases are already asleep.

> INTERVIEWER: Ok. Let me interrupt. Are the kids in the same room? Are they in the same bed?

BRAD: That was something I was going to mention. We recently upgraded our son's room to a . . . we call it "big-boy" room. So he's got a big-boy bed. At that point the children started to request being able to sleep together so we actually allowed them to do that. We periodically switch it around. There are seven days a week. So typically the days of the week get shifted to where one week on Monday they start in her room, and Tuesday, his room. The following Monday it switches back around, because there are seven days in the week. They sort of flip-flop back and forth.

Brad and Mandy had tried many strategies to keep the children out of their bed. However, they were in a bind because their daughter had frequent nightmares. In the end, it was the *children* who came up with a method that both accommodated their daughter's emotional needs and satisfied Brad and Mandy's desire to sleep alone. Mandy said they used their son as a kind of "calming tool." She joked, "It's terrible, but true. He's like a big, living teddy bear."

The children slept together in several other families. For example, David and Renee didn't have much space in their apartment so having the three boys sleep together was a practical thing to do. Renee describes it this way: "They slept the three of them on one mattress on the floor. And so what would happen was I would go and lay there and be there nursing them. If they were not nursing they were just used to sleeping with me on the floor. I would just go there and stay there until they fell asleep." David added, "Our youngest one had the easiest transition into sleeping without us because he was still sleeping with other people, his brothers, in the same room. So he didn't feel as scared or alone." Renee ended by saying, "He was excited, because he felt like a big boy sleeping with his brothers."

Sleeping Dynamics

As suggested above, co-sleeping is not static. Co-sleeping often involved the movement of children and parents from place to place. A poll conducted by the National Sleep Foundation found that in a substantial proportion of families, the children changed locations during the night. Families with infants (43 percent) moved the most, followed by toddlers and preschoolers (27 percent and 28 percent, respectively), and lastly school-aged children (14 percent).[5] Indeed, many of the parents I interviewed described how their children "crept," "strolled," and "wandered" in. Ariel is married and has two sons, ages six and three. She explained:

> If our [younger son] has fallen asleep first, then I will go put him in his bed and then I come back and sit with our [older son] until he falls asleep. If our [older son] falls asleep first, then I take our [younger son] and we go try to fall asleep somewhere else. No night is ever the same. Because sometimes if I'm lying with our [older son], our [younger son] will sneak into our room and lie down. If my husband is already in bed then he'll lie down with my husband and fall asleep in there if my husband doesn't push him back out. Sometimes our scenarios are different. Like last night I was gone so I came home and [my husband] had put them both to bed in their own beds but sometimes when I'm gone I come home and they're all sleeping in our bed.

The sleep patterns of families with more than one child were more unpredictable because the children tended to have different habits. Amy and her husband have four-year-old twin daughters. While their one daughter tended to stay in her own bed, the other was up much more often. Amy explained,

> Typically what happens is that our children go to bed in their own beds around 8:00. The plan is that they will spend the night in their own beds and wake up in their own beds in the

morning. Last night for example, [my daughter] came through about 2 a.m. and slid into bed with us. I stayed there with her for about an hour and she was very active. She moves around a lot and can be very disruptive. She thrashes around and kicks a lot in her sleep. It was about 3:30 when I cut my losses and went to sleep in her bed. It's different with [our other daughter]. She comes over much less frequently. She's less disruptive when she does. She'll get in on my side and just snuggle right in and be instantly asleep and not move. I find it somewhat less disruptive when she's the one to come over.

Similarly, Stacy described what it was like with a four-year-old and one-year-old:

The last few weeks we changed a little bit because I couldn't sleep well. I remember I took care of my son the first part of the night and the second part of the night my husband slept with [my son] in the same room but [with my son] in a bassinet. That lasted a few weeks and then he came back in the same room with me and my daughter. It was complicated! Then a few weeks later my daughter began to sleep in the same bed with my husband. Then, when my son was a year-and-a-half old I started my present job then I changed back to sleep with my daughter. My husband then slept together with my son.

What these interviews show is that co-sleeping is not always stable. A child's illness, trouble with nightmares, fear of storms, parents' travel, and work schedules all shape family sleeping arrangements as can a family crisis such as a death in the family or a divorce. Family sleeping arrangements also naturally evolved over time. The dynamic nature of family sleeping patterns calls into question many common assumptions about co-sleeping as the kids being either in the bed or out.

"SLIDING" INTO CO-SLEEPING

A main question for the parents in the study was why, when, and how they started co-sleeping with their children. As discussed in chapter 1, the conventional wisdom is that co-sleeping is a conscious choice. However, this was not the case for the majority of the parents in my study. Nearly all had purchased a crib and had a separate room designated for the child before their child was born. Danielle, who has a four- and six-year-old, did not plan to co-sleep. Like many of the parents in the study, she and her husband bought a crib and placed it in a separate room. But she says, "the night I brought [the baby] home from the hospital, I just couldn't bear to put her somewhere else so that room became a storage space." Sandra and her husband also did not intend to co-sleep. She said,

> We had bought a crib and we had the co-sleeper so the intent was going to be that he'd probably sleep in the co-sleeper until he was big enough and then he'd go in the crib. Because that's what we thought would work. And come to find out, that was not at all what happened! I mean, we had a brand-new crib and he didn't sleep in it once.

Similarly, Charlie and Gabby did not intend to sleep with their son but he has never slept anywhere else but with them in their bed. He told me, "We did buy a crib at a garage sale and it is still sitting in our garage. We never even put it together."

Intentional Co-Sleepers

Parents who decided to co-sleep with their child before their child's birth are referred to as *intentional co-sleepers*. Only a minority of the parents in the study described co-sleeping as a conscious choice. One was Julie who led an attachment parenting group in her community. She always planned to co-sleep with her children, at least as infants. With respect to her decision, she said, "A big benefit I have is that I always was a little bit more of an odd-ball. And people expected me to make bold choices. I mean, people don't bat an eye at me doing something weird. Whether it was weird babywearing, or home schooling, or some weird idea I had. I am heavily tattooed. Nobody's thought really anything of it."

Karen and Andy have two boys and had discussed co-sleeping before the birth of their first child. Andy said,

> Our midwife was very in favor of co-sleeping and probably encouraged us to do it. She probably just assumed we were doing it anyway because we're in the like hippiest, crunchiest circle of people you can imagine. Everyone we know does babywearing, and cloth diapering, co-sleeping, and breastfeeding their kids until they're like eight years old. Running around in wizard costumes . . . . [laughs]

Parents' feelings about co-sleeping also evolved as they experienced the realities of parenthood. Scarlett had not intended to co-sleep with her first child, but brought him into the bed at about eighteen months. She said,

> We had had such a good experience with [our first] since we started co-sleeping. I had since been in the attachment parenting group. The leader had an arms-reach co-sleeper that she offered. I knew I wanted to do some type of co-sleeping but I knew I didn't want my baby in the bed. So she let me borrow that and it was wonderful! It was just so much better as a newborn experience.

Reactive Co-Sleepers and Sliding into Co-Sleeping

Parents who do not intend to co-sleep are referred to as *reactive* co-sleepers. This was the case for many of the parents I interviewed. Bruce, a Marine who completed two tours in Iraq, stated,

"I would be the last person to be considered one of those, you know, 'hippie dads,' because I'm not like that. But, again it all comes back to the fact that she [his daughter] is my only weakness." Most parents were unable to pinpoint exactly when their child started sleeping with them. They described co-sleeping as a result of their child's constant crying, their child's having had a bad dream, or their child's having been sick or felt "lonely." In several cases, co-sleeping began when one of the parents started working at night. Linda describes a typical night with her two-year-old daughter.

> LINDA: I would say [my daughter] goes to bed between 8:30 and 9:00. We put her to bed in her room at first and then she gets up in the middle of the night. She's standing and says, "Mama, I hold you, I hold you." Then she comes to bed with us.

> INTERVIEWER: Does she cry or just say, "Mama"?

> LINDA: No. She's pretty much just like screaming. She's standing. "Mama! Mama! Mama! Mama, I hold you! I hold you!"

> INTERVIEWER: So it's pretty much every night?

> LINDA: Yeah. Pretty much every night.

Most said that they just kind of "fell into it." As mentioned earlier, Allison ended up buying double beds for all the children. When asked if co-sleeping was something she set out to do she said, "No. We were not like Doctor Sears followers. It just is what it is." Other parents said they didn't want to co-sleep but just gave up. Sarah, a single-mother, has two children, ages six and three. She talks about co-sleeping with her son and daughter, which began about the time of her divorce.

INTERVIEWER: When your little one comes in, does he go to sleep? Do you wake up?

SARAH: Half [of the] time I don't even realize he's coming in there. He doesn't bother waking me up. He doesn't say anything. He crawls over me, lies down, and is out.

INTERVIEWER: Before you can do anything?

SARAH: Kind of. I call him my "boomerang boy." I'll put him in his bed and about five minutes later [he] comes right back and falls asleep.

INTERVIEWER: What happens when you try to take him back to his bed?

SARAH: He'll lie down and then I think he just realizes [he's in bed]. I don't know how. He's got a sixth sense about where I am. I'll pick him up, put him back in his bed, he'll wake right up and come back. I mean it's all night! Until I just say, "Screw it, I'm going to sleep."

SLIDING OUT?

Most parents in the study lacked a clear plan to discontinue co-sleeping. Many had only loose plans to transition their child out of the bed such as "over the summer," "when he starts school," "when we move," or with the birth of the next child. Of his three-year-old son, Chris said, "We're kind of just letting it play out. I will say that there has been some tentative discussion that after the first of the year we'll set up his bed." Anthony and Samantha's response was similar. Samantha said, "For me, personally, it's while he's breastfeeding. It's the easiest thing, and I'm just sort of at his will of whenever he wants to wean into a bigger bed and that's when we'll do it. I just don't know." Anthony added, "Yeah. We have just sort of started to talk about that. I guess I sort of always defer to her on a lot of things like how long do people generally do this? I think we both kind of just want to play it by ear with him and hopefully he's not fourteen and sleeping in our bed." Charlie and his wife have a three-year-old son. When I asked if they had a specific time when they thought their son would move into his own space, he replied "I'm not going to be really motivated to do it quickly unless there's a [reason]. I can't imagine it really happening now that I think about it. I guess eventually we'll kick him out. But I can't imagine a kid ever saying 'I want out!' Similarly, Bruce and his wife have a three-year-old daughter. He said, "She's a very independent person, just like her mom, so it'll take care of itself. Now if she's thirteen, fourteen, fifteen, years old still wanting to sleep in the bed, then you know we've got an issue."

It would seem that just as families "slide into" co-sleeping, they expected they would "slide out." For example, some parents had older children who one day simply decided to sleep on their own. They talked about co-sleeping as a "learning process," that was "temporary," and that they would "monitor" the situation and "reevaluate." Many said co-sleeping was something they expected their child to grow out of. However, not all couples were willing to wait.

Attempts at Change

Parents used various strategies to get their children to stay in their own beds. I was able to interview only one parent in a same-sex relationship but her experience was similar to the other parents in the study. Gina and her wife have two children, a girl (age six) and a boy (age three). Gina described herself as mixed race, and she describes her spouse as Hispanic. She explains how they, especially Gina's spouse, are ambivalent about having the children share their bed. Nevertheless, they had not made any serious attempts to change the situation. They routinely discussed the issue in the daytime but did not have a clear plan aside from a "no co-sleeping" rule they rarely enforced. Gina described their nighttime routine below.

GINA: Typically our three-year-old goes to bed first, usually at least half an hour ahead of the six-year-old. He goes to bed in his own bed. We just moved, so we thought this was a chance to sort of remake our habits. So he has his own room now. He goes to sleep in his room. My daughter goes to sleep in her room. And then sometime in the night, between as early as eleven or as late as four, they join us in the bed.

INTERVIEWER: Can you describe how that works?

GINA: So one goes in between us, and whoever is second kind of slides alongside me. I kind of hold them so they don't flop out of the bed because we have [a] queen size bed, and we're not small people. So the kids kind of squeeze their way in.

INTERVIEWER: Okay. And who comes in first?

GINA: It is totally a surprise.

INTERVIEWER: You don't know who it's going to be?

GINA: I often don't know the kids are in the bed until I wake up in the morning. [My spouse] sort of interacts with them more at night. She usually knows who's where. I am often surprised by who it is.

INTERVIEWER: Do you ever try to take them back to their bed?

GINA: Maybe just once a month we'll sort of get fed up. We get to the point where we put them back into their bed, but not usually.

Tammy is a married mother with a seven-year-old son. Because she and her husband were planning to start trying for another child, they were anxious to get their son to sleep in his own bed. They were working hard to encourage their son to remain in his bed, offering incentives such as toys, but they found it difficult to be consistent with respect to taking him back to his own bed. Lately, they had been "giving in" to their son. She explains,

TAMMY: Usually like at one o'clock in the morning he'll come into our room and sleep with us the rest of the night. Now, he's seven, we would prefer for him to sleep in his own bed. We did try to bring him back every time and he'd usually end up back in our bed. Before, when I was working full-time nights, he would just come in and we would be too tired to take him back. Now, I'm currently working part-time nights. He'll ask to be taken back to his bed as long as one of us goes with him.

INTERVIEWER: To stay?

TAMMY: To stay. Because if we go back, then he'll go back. But for the most part, he will usually end up in our bed.

Rules and Rewards

Like Gina and Tammy, many parents had rules about co-sleeping but they found they were difficult to enforce. They described keeping their children out of their beds as a "battle," a "struggle," and a "challenge." Many parents created a regular nighttime routine with the main objective of getting their child to sleep in his or her own bed. Routines often included taking a bath, brushing teeth, reading stories, playing a game, saying prayers, and watching TV or videos. Even so, they found it was hard saying no, so their rules broke down over time. This was the case for Becky, who has two children ages five and three.

INTERVIEWER: So what have your discussions been lately, with her?

BECKY: Not much. I just get up and go on with the day because I haven't addressed it. Because I like sleep and I know that to break the pattern is going to require [my] being up in the night, dealing with her, and I honestly don't want to deal with it. And that's probably a bad answer but it's working for us right now and I feel like why try to change things? But she's getting older and I have been talking with her about it's time for you to get a big-girl bed. She knows her brother stays in the twin bed all night. And she has made a comment to me, "I don't want a big-girl bed because then I have to stay in my bed all night." I like to really use this to my advantage, when I've decided enough is enough maybe she'll think that the big bed means that she cannot sleep with me. But then I have to stick to my guns.

INTERVIEWER: So have you talked to your husband about it?

BECKY: No. He was very opposed to [my] sleeping with her from the beginning, but he has kind of just given up, because he sees that we're all getting sleep.

Mothers and fathers disagreeing about co-sleeping contributed to their lack of enforcement. Fathers were much less inclined to want their children in the bed. As Ariel, who has two children, explained, "Some nights I'm just very, very frustrated because they both take a long time to settle down. I try different things. We try to read books to settle them down but then my oldest one says, 'Mom can you please sit in bed by me?' or 'Can you lay with me?' I give in more than my husband. He's like, 'Go to Bed! Do not come out of your room!'"

Some parents rewarded their child for staying in his or her bed with a special privilege or prize. Several described trying to "bribe" their child. Others described their efforts as "positive reinforcement." These included nightlights, twinkle-lights, flashlights, music, and buying "transitional objects" to sleep with such as special blankets and stuffed animals. Kaylee is married and has a three-year-old son. She explained,

> We've tried a couple different things, and I'll tell you, I've not been strict about it. It's going to take a week solid just to get him in his own bed and I have a feeling he would have me up all night. And so I want to do it on a long weekend to kind of get it established. We did try it over this past month. We've been having him go in there and lay and watch a movie. He's got his little own TV on the floor, and so just to get him associated with the bed, because before he wouldn't touch his bed. He didn't want anything to do with his bed. And then we got him a dog. We thought we'd put the dog in his room and she'd sleep in there so then that way there was somebody else in there with him.

However, neither the dog nor any of these strategies worked. Julie incentivized her children to sleep in their beds by "trying to make things positive" and saying things like, "Oh, we've got a big-kid bed," and, "Here's the neat blanket with the characters you wanted on it.'" As long as their boys stayed in their beds during the week, Ariel and her husband allowed them in their bed on weekends as a "treat."

> We said on school nights you need to sleep in your bed. Weekends you can sleep in ours. They know if it's Friday night and Saturday night they get a "free pass" to either sleep in our bed or sometimes we lay blankets on the side of the bed and they both sleep on the floor. My husband can be kind of up and

down like it's okay sometimes. I mean he knows now, too, that on Sunday night it's back to your own bed because it's school the next morning.

Tammy and her husband wanted their seven-year-old son to sleep in his own bed in his own room. They tried many different strategies but nothing worked. She explains,

> He was very much at one point into space, so we even got the glow-in-the-dark stars and planets and stuff on the ceiling. The reason we got the bunk bed was because he wanted a bunk bed so we were thinking if he helped pick out the bed that he would stay in it. That made him easier with going to bed but he still got up in the middle of the night. And then, came the light thing. He was fine with the bathroom light up until this year. This year, when he started school is when we had to turn the lamp on in his bedroom all night. I asked him why and he said it was because he was scared of *The Grudge* [a horror movie]. Another little boy at school who apparently either heard of it or saw it, told him about it.

Parents often became discouraged. They talked about being too "permissive," giving their child "too much leeway" and being "weak." The next chapter explains parents' negative feelings about themselves in more detail.

Demographic Factors

Existing studies on co-sleeping tend to be based on homogeneous samples, specifically white, married, middle-class families. I therefore did my best to recruit parents from a variety of socio-demographic backgrounds. Although the majority of my participants were of this demographic, my sample is more diverse than those of previous researchers. My participants varied with respect to their education and income. They had a wide range of occupations. I interviewed both mothers and fathers. Some parents were stay-at-home parents and others worked. Among those who were employed there were both part- and full-time workers. Parents had a variety of work schedules, as did their spouses and partners. My sample included single, cohabiting, divorced, and remarried parents. The participants practiced a number of different religions and attended services at different frequencies. I interviewed black, Hispanic, and Asian parents. This diversity allowed me to explore whether and how these sources of variation may be related to their sleep patterns.

Gender

Of my fifty-one participants, thirteen were fathers. One of my most striking findings was the similarity of mothers' and fathers' descriptions. Although in American society the care of young children is typically assigned to mothers, the fathers in my study were able to describe their families' sleep routines in great detail. They expressed the same joys and frustrations. There was little evidence of gender-of-parent differences in their reports. Similarly, I found no differences in co-sleeping behavior in families with boys, girls, and both boys and girls. Boys and girls were equally likely to desire to sleep with their parents, and the gender of the child was not mentioned by any parent as a factor in letting them in the bed or wanting them out, or as a factor in any other aspect of their particular sleeping arrangements.

Race and Ethnicity

I interviewed a number of parents who were from countries, outside the United States, where co-sleeping is more common. Renee grew up in Brazil and was part of a large family with a small house. She explained, "It was a big family, so I slept with one of my brothers until I was eight years old. And our bed was in my parents' bedroom, because the other rooms were taken with one for the boys, one for the girls. We were the two younger ones.

And so my brother was sixteen, and I was eight, and we were still sleeping together, the two of us." Evelyn grew up in Mexico. She said,

> So at the beginning, my parents were living with us just how to teach us how to be parents. You know, the basic 101s. We were using the little bassinet, and my mom was kind of confused. She kind of got offended. She was like, "Why don't you want him sleeping with me or with you guys?" I think our parents kind of looked at us like we were a little crazy, you know? When we tried to explain why we did it, because of SIDS, they kind of just looked at us like, "We don't know what you're talking about."

Janessa is from China and described how as a child she slept with her mother and sisters. She said the other Chinese mothers in her apartment complex also co-sleep. I interviewed another couple who grew up in China, Stacy and Walter. Stacy said her earliest memory was that she slept with her sister and mother and father in one big bed. Walter, who did not live with his parents growing up, slept with his grandmother. However, while the non-white parents in my study seemed less concerned about co-sleeping than the white parents, they did not necessarily express a greater desire to co-sleep.

Employment

Some parents had work schedules that encouraged co-sleeping—specifically when fathers had long work hours. This was the case for Valerie. When I asked her why she slept with her younger daughter she replied, "She's just spoiled rotten. She'd say, 'Mommy, I wanna sleep with you guys.' And [my husband] worked nights a lot of times so it was like, 'Oh you can come sleep with me because dad's not home.'"

Family Structure

Few studies have examined co-sleeping in different family structures. Although several studies have examined co-sleeping among single mothers, they did not investigate divorce or the transition from a two-parent to a one-parent household. Similarly, there have been no studies of co-sleeping in cohabiting or stepfamilies, which is a problem given the dramatic increase in nontraditional family forms. Therefore, many questions remain. Do children sleep in the same bed as their mother's boyfriend? When co-sleeping parents remarry, do they still allow their children in the bed? The answers are complex.

The following comes from Sharon, who is a single mother of a twelve-year-old daughter. She and her daughter began co-sleeping after Sharon's divorce and subsequent move to a new home. When her daughter was younger, they slept together nearly every night. Their pattern of co-sleeping evolved over time. Sharon explained that although her daughter is getting older and comes into her room less often, they still sometimes co-sleep. Although she generally doesn't mind this, it sometimes presented problems.

INTERVIEWER: Would you say that occasionally it still might be the case that she would come and sleep with you or that you would sleep with her?

SHARON: Occasionally. I think it was just last week that she tried to. She tried to crawl in bed with me twice last week.

INTERVIEWER: Ok, and what happened?

SHARON: Um, it was not a good time for her to. [*laughs*]

INTERVIEWER: Ok, were you alone?

SHARON: No, I was not. [*laughs*] It was one of the rare occasions when somebody was actually in my room and she just happened to choose that night to come in. She tried to go in there the next night, too, but I decided that it was time for her to stay in her own room at twelve.

Sharon's daughter was not happy, but eventually stopped asking to sleep with her mom. In the book, *The Maternal Bed: Mothering and Ambivalence*, Wendy Hollway cautions that when there is a new partner the child may feel excluded and resentful, in that they realize that they no longer occupy a privileged status.[6] She says this may create anxiety and exacerbate fears. Children can be torn between desiring maternal comfort in the night and facing a possibly resented and unwelcome "intruder." One mother with a new boyfriend allowed him to sleep in the same bed as her child. Jenna is a twenty-six-year-old single mother of a four-month-old.

INTERVIEWER: You had mentioned that you're in a new relationship right now. Is co-sleeping something that has come up?

JENNA: [My boyfriend] came and visited me about two weeks ago and he did sleep in the bed with us. The baby did sleep in between the two of us. It didn't bother me, and it didn't bother him. But he was so nervous about the baby being in between us that he didn't sleep very well.

INTERVIEWER: He was worried about hurting the baby?

JENNA: He was worried about rolling over on the baby. But, it doesn't bother him. One day I came home from running errands and they were sleeping together. He was rolled up with him in his arms sleeping together. It was one of [those] picture-perfect things. It was pretty sweet. So it doesn't bother him and he loves [my baby].

Danielle is divorced and has a four- and a six-year-old. When she had her second child, her two children slept in the bed with her and her husband. Now divorced from her children's father, Danielle has a system in which her children alternate sleeping in her bed. She says, "They each have two nights and I have one night to myself." When they are visiting their dad they all sleep, "on a big mattress on the floor of his room." Julie's children slept with her more often after her divorce. She explained, "When I divorced I assumed that everyone's coming back [to my room]. It was a time of crisis and that kind of thing. I had a king on the floor and a queen on the floor and everybody was welcome and for a while; everybody came."

Although I did not have many single, divorced, or cohabiting parents in my sample, I could find no evidence that any of them had concerns or worries about their child's sleeping with an unrelated adult. I examined the role of other factors including the ages and number of the children in the family (discussed previously). Neither parents' age, level of education, occupation, religious affiliation, religious attendance, nor income appeared to be related to the particular habits of co-sleeping families.

CONCLUSION

The descriptions, by parents in the study, of their families' sleeping patterns build upon previous research regarding the nature and origins of co-sleeping in families. Similar to previous research, some parents in my study were *intentional* co-sleepers. Co-sleeping was part of their overall approach to parenting, and several specifically mentioned that they practiced attachment parenting. Likewise, some of the parents in this study were *reactive co-sleepers*, who co-sleep in reaction to children's nighttime problems, such as nightmares, as was the case for Mandy and Brad. Their feelings about co-sleeping were substantially more mixed.

While they discussed many advantages of co-sleeping (such as the opportunity to cuddle, read stories, and talk), they mentioned just as many disadvantages (being awakened, kicked, pushed out). Reactive co-sleepers tended to "slide" or "drift" into co-sleeping, commonly referred to as *sliding versus deciding*.[7] Contrary to popular beliefs about family life, many important life transitions and family processes are the result of *indecision* as opposed to decision. Cohabitation and childlessness are two well-known examples. Co-sleeping is another.

Parents who were intentional co-sleepers facilitated co-sleeping by, for instance, buying large beds for everyone in the family. Reactive co-sleepers had at some point attempted to keep their children in their own beds. This group tended to have more of a plan as to how (e.g., offering rewards) and when (e.g., with the birth of the second child) this would come about, and were much more likely to follow through. Although reactive co-sleepers sometimes had a plan, they tended to be lax in terms of enforcement. Some reported that they currently were "taking a break" from the plan. Some had given up on the idea altogether, hoping their children would eventually stop wanting to sleep with them. A lack of communication with their spouse, differences of opinion as to whether to allow the children in the bed, not having strong feelings for or against co-sleeping, and sheer exhaustion were among the reasons for not following through.

This chapter presented parents' descriptions of a "typical night" in their home. However, these descriptions indicate that there *is* no typical. There was a great deal of variation in sleeping patterns across families and variation within families. Moreover, sleep patterns were not consistent over time, often changing on a nightly basis. They were affected by practical issues such as work schedules and the layout of the family home. Furthermore, the children's role should not be underestimated. Children could be highly involved in the negotiations, sometimes coming up with creative solutions (such as sleeping with a sibling). In other families, children thwarted their parents' plans by sneaking into their bed or room without their knowledge.

These parents' descriptions revealed a number of misconceptions about co-sleeping. First, co-sleeping is different than bed-sharing. Co-sleeping is complex and dynamic and encompasses a variety of arrangement, locations, and movements. Second, contrary to popular assumptions about co-sleeping, parents do not necessarily choose to co-sleep. Rather, many parents "slide" into co-sleeping after their children are born. Third, co-sleeping is not always the idea of parents. A family's sleeping arrangements result from a mix of parent, child, and environmental factors.

Because previous research has focused mostly on mothers' co-sleeping with infants and very young children who are not yet mobile, such variations in family sleep patterns had not been previously documented. Probably the closest researchers have come to understanding the details of family sleep behavior among families with a wider age range of children comes from research by David Maume, who studied the sleep patterns of married couples in which one spouse worked the night shift.[8] My findings are consistent with the results of their study in that seeing to the needs of children was a common reason for their sleep disruptions.

Another goal of the book was to examine the extent to which these patterns varied by the social and demographic characteristics of families. Probably the most important source of variation was children's ages. Because previous research has focused mostly on mothers co-sleeping with infants who are obviously not mobile, differences in the sleep patterns of families with infants, toddlers, and school-aged children had not been previously documented. Aside from age, few social or demographic variables seemed to matter. A wide variety of families co-slept. While several of the parents in the study saw themselves as "hippies," the vast majority described themselves as typical parents.

My interviews revealed a complex and dynamic "bedtime story" in that family interaction does not end when the lights go out. Rather, this chapter shows a great deal of diversity in sleep patterns both between families and within families and inventive strategies that either facilitate or prevent co-sleeping. As the number of dual-earner families rises, time-strapped parents are increasingly juggling work and family roles that can bleed into the wee hours.[9] My interviews suggest that parents don't simply abandon their responsibilities at bedtime. Rather, parenting continues throughout the night.

Now that we know something about the nighttime activities of co-sleeping families, we will get parents' perspectives on co-sleeping, including their feelings about their sleeping arrangements, their level of satisfaction and/or dissatisfaction with them, specific changes they would like to make, and their future plans regarding co-sleeping as their children age.

3

PARENTS' PERSPECTIVES ON CO-SLEEPING

INTERVIEWER: What word or phrases would you use to describe your feelings about your family's sleeping arrangements?

JODY (married with three children ages eight, six, and sixteen months): Honestly a lot of the times it's "frustration." Frustration that your child is struggling. Frustration that I would like to go to bed and sleep all the way through the night without getting up for something. I would just like to have a restful night's sleep and know that everyone's okay. We've let them cry it out. We've let them scream. Even if they fall asleep they'll only stay asleep for like fifteen minutes. It's kind of a running joke in our family that [our older son] is eight and I feel as though I haven't slept in eight years.

Our society's chief concern around co-sleeping has generally been the potential negative impact of co-sleeping on children, which may be because traditionally the family as an institution is assumed to have a "top-down" organizational structure. The conventional wisdom is that the transmission of values, attitudes, and behavior flows from parents to children exclusively with children as the "receptors" or even "victims" of family dynamics. Yet, children also shape their interactions with adult family members, and adult family members' relationships with each other, operating from the "bottom-up" so to speak.[1]

This chapter highlights how co-sleeping affects parents. For example, numerous studies have shown that parenting a child with a physical or mental disability can take a toll on parents. Even without a disability, raising children can be physically and emotionally draining. Forty-five years ago social scientist Alice Rossi wrote that the *transition to parenthood* is difficult for several reasons. With little experience, first-time parents must abruptly assume twenty-four-hour duty caring for a fragile, dependent baby. Babies interrupt parents' sleep, work, and leisure time.[2] As one new mother said, "You have to run to bathe yourself because the child is going to wake up."[3]

It is well-known that American parents, especially mothers, are both exhausted and "stressed out." Numerous studies indicate lower levels of psychological well-being among parents than non-parents.[4] American culture promotes the idea that parents are solely responsible for their children's successes, as well as their failures, which contributes to parental stress. Yet, parenting involves a "complex interplay among parent, child, and situation" and factors beyond parents' control.[5] Moreover, it is often everyday aspects of parenting that cause parents the most stress, such as the daily hassles of figuring out what to have for dinner, having to miss work to stay home with a sick child, being stuck in traffic, and, as it turns out, *getting the children to sleep*.[6] Younger parents have more trouble coping with day-to-day stressors, as do parents in nontraditional families, single parents, and cohabitors.[7] And as men's involvement in parenting increases, understanding their perspectives has become crucial, especially because men experience stress differently than women.[8]

Chapter 2 described the sleeping arrangements and nighttime activities of families who co-sleep. Drawing on interview questions about how parents experience co-sleeping, positive and negative emotions they had about co-sleeping, and what they saw as advantages and disadvantages of co-sleeping, this chapter highlights how parents feel about co-sleeping. This chapter also highlights differences in parents' perspectives based on their gender, race and ethnicity, and family structure. First, I provide parents' descriptions of the benefits of co-sleeping.

BENEFITS OF CO-SLEEPING

Practicality

All the parents in the study identified at least some positive aspects of co-sleeping. Many emphasized its practicality. For them, co-sleeping simply "made sense." For example, Gabby grew up in Mexico and has a three-year-old daughter. She's pregnant with another child. She said,

> In my culture the native woman all co-sleep. Because I've seen it, I feel somewhat attached to it. Otherwise when I see people doing it here in this country it's kind of like, "Oh, okay." It's nothing out of the ordinary for me. It's not that I'm not attracted to it because it's a philosophy. It's just that it's great. It's convenient. It's efficient.

Other parents viewed co-sleeping as "no big deal." For example, Bruce said, "I was in the military. I can sleep anywhere. It really doesn't matter. I don't mind sleeping with her. I'm half-way asleep anyway so I just want what's easiest." Many parents said co-sleeping helped them and their child get more sleep. Jenna is a single mother of a four-month-old son. When I asked about the positive side of co-sleeping she said,

Positives? I get a lot of sleep. As opposed to getting up and having to listen to my monitor. When I first had him I was constantly listening to him breathe. Because with newborns they'll stop breathing for like eight to ten seconds. And it freaks you out but there's nothing wrong with him. After I got to that point I just decided that we're just going to try it and it worked. He gets a lot of good sleep.

Snuggling

By far, "cuddling" and "snuggling" with their children was listed as the most positive aspect of co-sleeping. Diana and Paul's responses were typical. When I asked about the advantages of co-sleeping, Diana said, "I think probably the connection with [my son]. I think it's a little bit more family time for us since we don't get a whole lot. It's just snuggling. I like snuggling, you know? It's just nice." Paul agreed. He said, "We don't like to set him down. We love holding him. I think that's got something to do with it. I think that we both enjoy that he sleeps in the bed with us, even though I know in the back of my mind it's probably going to be a lot harder to get him to sleep in his own bed."

Ariel's sons are six and three. She explained,

> I am a cuddle-person and I don't mind doing that until they actually fall asleep. I've gotten hit in the head many times by flying arms and legs and feet, but once they're sleeping, I like it. In the morning when they're in there and if we don't have to get up I like that little cuddle time. They're also boys. They're not always going to want to do that. As long as they want to do it, it's all right because I know someday they're not.

Quality Time

Nighttime also provided an opportunity for parents to spend "quality time" with their children. This was especially true of parents who worked long hours or who were away from home during the day. Scarlett works full-time and has two children, ages eight and two. She said, "I work all day and then I get home and it's dinner and spelling and piano practice. It's really a nice time to connect. At two-and-a-half, she's just really busy playing all the time so one of our few times to cuddle is at night when we're going to sleep and in the morning before we get up." Kaylee, who has a three-year-old son, agreed. She said, "I work all the time, so when I get home it's like all I want to do is spend time with him. I feel like when he's in the bed with me I'm still getting to spend that time with him regardless [of] if he's sleeping. I'm still getting to give him that love and attention that I don't get to give him all day."

That co-sleeping allowed quality time with the children was especially true for fathers. Lisa said of her husband, "Even just the other day spontaneously he said, 'it's so great to wake up and see my beautiful girls!' They're so little and they cuddle with me in the night. He's gone to work all day and so this is extra time he gets with them." Anthony and Samantha have a three-month-old son. She said, "On the weekends when [our son] wakes up and sees [his dad] he's just like, 'Ah! Daddy, you're in bed!' He just lights up and it's the coolest thing that Daddy's there. It's really cool to have those Saturday and Sunday mornings together and play with him in bed." Many fathers in my study used co-sleeping as a way to spend extra time with their children. William Sears in his book *Becoming a Father* states that "nighttime should be a time for fathers and children to enjoy each other."[9]

Co-Sleeping Is Natural

A consistent theme throughout the interviews was that co-sleeping is a natural and normal thing to do. Anthony and Samantha have a three-month-old son. She said, "To me it was the most natural thing to sleep with him. I look forward to going to bed now. It's not like, 'Oh, I'm going to be up all night. This is going to be awful.' It's like just a really great bonding time with him." Chris agreed. "It works out. We do it because it's what's easy. It feels comfortable. It feels right."

A number of parents mentioned that humans evolved to co-sleep. This was the case for Amanda, who has a nine-month-old daughter.

> INTERVIEWER: When you said that you heard co-sleeping is bad, is there anyone in particular who might have said, "Oh, that's not a good idea?"

> AMANDA: I think the first time I heard that message was in the hospital. I'm holding my brand new baby and they're like, "Now don't fall asleep with that baby!"

> INTERVIEWER: The nurses?

> AMANDA: Yes. I'm exhausted and had just given birth and she's screaming every time I put her down next to me in this hospital thing. It was so miserable! All of my instincts are telling me to pick up the baby! She's crying! They're not supposed to be alone! Evolutionarily we did not leave babies alone. And the nurses are saying, "No, you can't do that." So I'm going: what do I do? The nurses are telling me this isn't safe!

Linda, who has a two-year-old son, shared Amanda's feelings. She said,

> I try to tell folks that babies are the greatest example of what our ancestors were like because they don't know anything. If you let your baby cry for extended periods of time they're going to be eaten by a predator. There are reasons why you keep your babies close and you don't let them cry. You wear them because you know they couldn't outrun the mastodons or

whatever. They have not evolved out of those needs. I mean, if we said, "Oh, I'm going to let my baby sleep in the cave off by herself," they would be dead.

Many parents noted that co-sleeping is widely practiced in other cultures. Linda said, "We've been socialized to believe that babies are supposed to sleep by themselves. This is a really Western perspective. In other places kids don't have individual rooms." Rosalie, who's from Brazil, agreed saying, "I thought that it was more of a cultural thing than anything else because all the comments I heard while in the U.S. were more negative than positive, like, 'you've got to teach the kid to sleep in his own bed.' If I were talking to someone from my family, it would be the most natural thing in the world. To this day my nephews and nieces [in Brazil] just go to their parents' bed."

Security and Comfort

Many parents felt insecure about having their children apart from them at night. This was especially true of parents with infants. Amanda, who has a nine-month-old daughter, explained, "It's a complicated issue that's been made very simple. Yeah, babies die of SIDS in co-sleeping situations but they also die of SIDS in cribs. I think it's been made to look much more clear-cut than it actually is. I think some research actually shows there's less chance of your baby dying of SIDS when you're sleeping next to her." Parents were themselves comforted by sleeping with their children. Kaylee, who has a three-year-old son, said, "To me I think sometimes it's just kind of like my security blanket. He would be my security blanket because I've done it for so long that it's just so natural to me." Chris's response was similar. He said, "There were several reasons why we co-slept: for the sake of convenience and from a breastfeeding perspective so that [my wife] didn't have to get up. I also loved the cuddling. Just being there and waking during the night and seeing him and hearing him breathing and those kinds of the things. So, it was very comforting for me." Jenna, mother of a four-month-old son, said, "I think I decided that I wanted to co-sleep because of what I went through. I got walked out on as a single mom when I was five months pregnant. I was kind of dealing with having to heal myself from that and having him with me just made it feel better I guess."

DISADVANTAGES OF CO-SLEEPING

All the parents in the study identified negative aspects of co-sleeping, regardless of whether they intended to co-sleep or viewed co-sleeping as positive and beneficial.

Accomplishing Sleep

Nighttime is generally thought of as a time to relax, rest, and recharge, but for parents with young children, not necessarily. For all the parents in the study, getting the children to sleep through the night required that they engage in a great deal of physical and emotional labor. Nighttime was a busy, productive time. In addition to feeding, nighttime activities included soothing crying children, returning children to their rooms, moving over for and repositioning children, and taking children to the bathroom. These activities required parents to be awake and alert.

Sleep was something parents *accomplished*, not unlike getting the family up, dressed, and off to work or school. A "good" night was when everyone in the family got high-quality, continuous sleep. A "bad" night was when parents, children, or both, did not—when sleep was disrupted by crying, calling out, and the pitter-patter of little feet. Many parents saw getting their children to sleep in their own beds *and staying there* in the same way they saw getting them to brush their teeth and eating their vegetables. Parents often defined co-sleeping as "the situation," "an issue," or "a problem" that they "managed," "dealt with," or "handled." When describing their feelings, many of them used words like "frustrated," "anxious," "uncertain," and even "desperate." Many parents framed co-sleeping as something "bad," referring to a "bad night" or a "bad time," or that their child was a "bad sleeper" with "bad habits." Or, that they were "bad parents" and that co-sleeping was a "bad idea." These themes are described in more detail below.

Working the Night Shift

Several parents in the study specifically noted that parenting does not end "when the lights go out." Nighttime was often described in terms of work. Many parents used work-related phrases such as being "on the clock" or "in the trenches." Lisa is married and has two girls ages six and two. She described it this way:

> When they're so little we want to be there to help them. For example, when your kid wakes up in the night and they're throwing up. We know. Everybody in the family knows immediately that the child is sick and they need to be washed up. The sheets need to be changed and it's "all hands on deck" as opposed to parents who are at the other end of the house. Their kids wake up with puke in their hair. And I don't want to do that! It's just not the right choice for our family. We really are twenty-four-hour parents.

Julie is a single mother who has three biological children and two special-needs children adopted through the foster care system. She said, "I have a policy that you don't get to 'clock-out' when it's dark outside. I'm mothering twenty-four hours a day. If somebody needs me they're welcome to come to me in the night."

This can be tiring for parents, however. Linda is married and has a two-year-old daughter. She explained,

> Right now the challenge is when we come to her room and she's already standing in her crib and if I say lay back down she's not going to do that. Because we've tried that. Even if I sit next to her crib and try and rub her back through the crib slots she's not having that either. If she wakes up in the middle of the night then at least one of us has to lie next to her.

That children need to be "trained" or "taught" how to sleep is not a new idea. Richard Ferber, considered the originator of the so-called "cry it out" method, contends that the idea that some children are "bad sleepers" and that "nothing can be done about it" is rarely true and that real sleep problems in children are actually quite rare. He advocated simple interventions to keep children in their beds, such as consistent bedtimes, daytime (e.g., naps, meals) and nighttime (e.g., reading stories) routines, and limit setting (e.g., limiting television viewing, reducing nighttime feedings). He argues that that is good for children and parents alike. Studies have found a consistent bedtime routine to be associated with a more positive mood (less tension, anger, and fatigue) among mothers with infants and toddlers [10] Several parents in the study mentioned having tried such sleep-training methods.

Parental Ambivalence

About half of the parents were asked to rate their feelings about co-sleeping on a scale from one to ten, with a lower score indicative of more negative feelings. Their scores ranged from two to ten and a score of five was most common. Responses were skewed toward the higher end of the scale: fourteen parents had scores greater than five compared to only five parents who had scores under five. Kaylee's answer was typical:

INTERVIEWER: On a scale from one to ten, where one is "I really don't like co-sleeping and want it to stop," and ten is "I really like co-sleeping and I want it to continue," where would you fall?

KAYLEE: I'd say I'm smack dab in the middle because like I said I enjoy that time with him. It's going to be hard for me to give it up, but then again I know that he needs time away from mommy.

A number of parents had difficultly answering this question and had trouble settling on a score. Jody said,

> I would say like a three. On the lower end. I wouldn't say a one because for me as a mother and for little ones there's something wonderful about curling up with your baby and spending time with them. But as far as having a child in your bed, I would say I'm a one. I don't really want my kids sleeping with me. But I range in the three or four—of really enjoying the time that I did co-sleep when they were babies. I did enjoy that portion of it.

Janet said of her three-year-old daughter, "She would talk to us and stroke our faces and say, 'Momma, I love you.' I mean, it's sweet but I don't want to hear that at 3 a.m." Gina's response was similar. "I feel a little conflicted. Most of the time I feel like they're going to be independent from us the whole rest of their lives and I feel like this lovely, sweet intimacy is something that we should savor, except when they're kicking my back."

All of the parents in the study expressed some degree of ambivalence about co-sleeping. In her book, *Torn in Two: The Experience of Maternal Ambivalence*, Rozsika Parker argues that parenting *requires* some degree of ambivalence.[11] She says in order to create emotionally healthy and self-reliant adults parents need to simultaneously nurture their children and push them to be independent. Nevertheless, she argues that American society sentimentalizes clinging while stigmatizing pushing.

In American culture, the self-sacrifice is what makes a "good mother." Mothers are expected to be completely devoted to their children and put their children's and family's needs above their own. It is assumed that pregnancy and early parenthood is a wholly fulfilling, joyous time for mothers; feelings of irritation, frustration, and anger are not allowed.[12] The presumption of self-sacrifice in the presence of what is normal ambivalence about motherhood can be very damaging and has been found to be associated with guilt, stress, anxiety, and, more seriously, antenatal and postpartum depression. Pregnant women and new mothers can be so ashamed and frightened of their feelings that they do not seek help. For example, fearing the effects on the fetus ("I could never forgive myself," "I couldn't do that to my child"), some women may refuse anti-depressants or go off their medication during pregnancy to the detriment of their own well-being.[13]

"Mommy guilt," as it is popularly known, was common among the mothers in my study. On the one hand, mothers felt guilty for letting their child sleep with them. Kaylee blames herself for co-sleeping:

> A lot of it's my fault that he still sleeps with us; it truly is. It's something I have to do and it's going to be hard for me. That's probably why I keep pushing if off. It's hard. When he's done it for so long and it's just a natural routine for us, it's going to be weird when the time comes when he is not in the bed anymore. I mean I know it needs to be done. It's not healthy. It really isn't healthy for a family.

On the other hand, many mothers felt guilty for *not* letting their child sleep with them. Sharon is a single mother of a twelve-year-old daughter. She described the process of transitioning her daughter out of her bed as "bittersweet." She said, "I think I felt a little guilty that I wasn't sleeping with her, but then there's a part of me that feels like she is growing up and she really shouldn't be doing this anymore." Becky has two children, a son and a daughter. She said:

> Sometimes I feel kind of bad because he'd come in the room in the night and I just make him go back to bed. And if he's upset I'll go with him or I'll give him a hug and I try to give him a reward in the morning. He's really into video games and I let him play on my iPad for a few minutes in the morning when he wakes up. Sometimes my daughter wants the reward. She has asked before, can I play the iPad? And I say, "No, you didn't stay in your bed all night."

Crystal, who has two- and four-year-old daughters, felt similarly. She said,

> We envisioned that we would be kind of the parents that you would see in a magazine with the crib in the other room or something, and my husband's family was definitely not co-sleeping or breastfeeding advocates. My family just didn't talk about it so we didn't know that these things were even possible. Before we had [our daughter] sleeping in our room, she was screaming for seven months, and the stress that we felt was huge—just huge. We tried everything, reading books to her, holding hands with her through the bars of her crib, or whatever we could do, but not picking her up. It just felt, it just felt wrong. And then as soon as I started sleeping with her, it was working. I think we just always felt guilt about either having her in her crib or me sleeping in a different arrangement. We don't really have the guilt now that we've just kind of made it a family thing.

Ambivalence was experienced by both mothers and fathers. This makes sense given how dramatically fathers' roles have changed in the last few decades. As more mothers have joined the workforce, fathers' role as the sole breadwinner in the family has declined with their increasing responsibility for the care and nurturance of children. While many fathers enjoy this new role, expectations still exist that they be strong disciplinarians who set limits, and encourage their children to go "out into the world." Stephen Frosh refers to fathers' confusion, worry, and inconsistency with respect to parenting as a "crisis of masculinity."[14] Andy, who has two boys ages two and four, expressed this sentiment. He said this about co-sleeping:

> It makes me feel very powerless. Every single day I have no control over even getting my kids put down to bed. Sometimes I feel like we've given up so much for this process of parenting. We've given up our jobs. We've given up our life savings. We've lost so much. That's a bad way to look at it, but we've given up *everything* for this process. Would we have been any worse off if we could have done things in a way that was more deliberate, drawing a line and keep this for ourselves? We need to keep ourselves sane in this one way. And so we can't have kids sleeping in the bed. I mean, I don't know. It just wears me out sometimes. I just don't know entirely if this style of parenting is worth it. Sometimes I feel like I would be a better father if I had a happier relationship with my wife. That we got to be together as a couple more often and I wasn't exhausted all the time from getting kicked in the crotch all night. [*laughs*]

Humor

The use of humor was common throughout the interviews. Parker argues that this is the only way mothers can safely "confess" their ambivalence about their children.[15] Both the mothers and fathers in the study laughed a lot during the interviews and often made jokes at their children's expense. Valerie playfully referred to her daughter as "spoiled rotten." Andy, from above, said his parents were "worried about my sanity." Linda said, "This baby is killing me!" Several parents mentioned being "driven crazy" by sleeping with their kids. When asked what her ideal sleeping situation would be, Stacy, who is originally from China, laughingly exclaimed, "Each person, own room. One person, each room!"

Worries and Concerns

Parents who were co-sleeping had many worries and concerns. Mandy, who has two children ages five and three, expresses this overall sentiment. She said, "I wish there was a manual and I could know if I was doing the right thing. I worry that years down the road we will pay for the decisions that we've made. I think we won't know for a while if this was the right thing to do. In trying to have my daughter face her fears and get used to sleeping by herself." Worries about co-sleeping were in two main areas: children's physical safety and their social and emotional health.

Worries about Their Child's Physical Safety

First and foremost was parents' concern over their child's physical safety and primarily that co-sleeping would increase their child's risk of SIDS (sudden infant death syndrome). Every single parent in the study mentioned SIDS as the most worrisome aspect of co-sleeping (I took care never to mention SIDS myself). As discussed later in chapter 5, the parents in the study were regularly on the receiving end of negative comments from others about co-sleeping, especially related to SIDS; such comments served to only magnify their worries. Anthony, who has a three-month-old child, put it this way: "Our society is pretty fear-based, like with *Dateline* episodes saying that your kids are going to explode, you know? Like, if you don't do things exactly the way you're supposed to, your kid's going to suffocate."

Fathers in particular expressed a lot of concern about their child's physical safety. This is consistent with the traditional male role of the father as the "protector" of the family, and perhaps because men have less experience than women with caring for young children. Anthony said, "I think we were both hypervigilant. But me personally, I was pretty terrified of falling asleep and dropping him somewhere. Falling into a couch, that kind of thing." He didn't even like having the cat in the bed. He said, "I suppose that was just something that was on my mountain of paranoia at the very beginning, like the old wives' tale about the cat sleeping on the baby. Which I don't think is true, but we made sure the cat wasn't in the bed."

Nevertheless, it was the mothers who generally tended to the children at night. Many mothers talked about being more "in tune" with their children's needs. Jody and Matthew have three children, ages eight, six, and sixteen months. She said of her husband, "I think it's me more so than Matthew who is a very sound sleeper. He does hear the kids, but I don't know if it's a cliché to say as a mom I have more anxiety if I hear a cough or I'm like, 'Oh, does that sound croupy?' Or, 'Oh, I just heard that.' That's just kind of how I am."

Worries about Their Child's Social and Emotional Health

Parents also mentioned that they were concerned about how co-sleeping would affect their children's psychological development. They worried about "spoiling" their child and that they would become "over-attached" and "clingy." Interestingly, several parents, who themselves co-slept, judged other co-sleeping parents quite harshly. Jody described her sister's children:

> They're unbelievably needy. The seven-year-old is still probably the neediest and still does not sleep by himself. He gets up, comes down to their bed, crawls in their bed and stays with them the entire night. Then the other kid comes down. So literally they will have three kids in their bed sleeping with them the entire night. I would say two of the three are plenty

old enough to be on their own in their beds and they all stay with them almost every night. I think that's crazy. But that's my opinion.

Parents also were worried that co-sleeping might cause their children to have sleep problems such as not ever being able to sleep on their own. Although Sharon liked snuggling with her twelve-year-old daughter, she said, "I think it's better for a child to be able to self-sooth so it worries me, you know? That she's going to jump into bed with somebody somewhere because she's not accustomed to sleeping alone." Mandy, whose five-year-old daughter sleeps with her three-year-old son, said, "We worry about damaging them in some way. My son would probably sleep just fine if we never brought him into the room with his sister. So are we taking something away from them by not giving them their own private little area or are we just making problems?"

Charlie expressed similar feelings. He said, "I understand the benefits. But the other side of it is that I don't want him to grow up too attached where he is afraid to go out and experience life, you know?"

Others were concerned that co-sleeping would be a "hard habit to break" and that they would never be able to get their child out of their bed. Linda, who has a two-year-old daughter, worried about this. She said, "You always kind of wonder like, what am I starting? Like am I starting any bad habits?" Similarly, Kaylee, who has a three-year-old son, said, "I'm worried if we don't get him out pretty soon it's going to be harder. I know my older sister, her little boy is seven, and he's still sleeping with her! I don't want that to happen."

None of the parents I interviewed mentioned the concerns that are commonly discussed in articles about co-sleeping, such as the worry that co-sleeping would cause marital difficulties, that children might witness intercourse, or that the child might be sexually abused.

CONCLUSION

The experiences and voices of real parents are important to fully understand the implications of co-sleeping for families. The parents interviewed for this book identified many advantages of co-sleeping. These same parents also identified many disadvantages. A constant theme running through the interviews was that of ambivalence. They expressed feelings of joy, comfort, and love, but also anxiety, frustration, and stress.

Why, then, do they do it? Probably the same reason that parents choose to have children at all in a culture that is not particularly "family friendly." American parents face many challenges. They work long hours and take few vacations. Only a tiny percentage of companies provide paid or extended parental leave. Reasonably priced, high-quality childcare is hard to find and relatives often live far away. Studies have found that rather than making parents happier, children actually reduce life satisfaction. While the *prospect* of having a child and pregnancy is associated with an increase in personal happiness, personal happiness drops right after the birth. The size of the negative effect depends on factors such as the gender, age, level of education of the parents, and income, with older and better-off parents and fathers experiencing less of a drop. One study found that the negative effect of the first child can be so strong it may deter couples from having additional children.[16]

My findings related to the stresses of new parenthood are not unlike those of previous research. For example, in a study of Mexican-born women living in the United States, a mother talks about being a new parent: "The baby cried a lot. I didn't understand why, and I started to cry. . . . It's not like you think, you don't sleep the same, you don't eat the same. It was all different." It may help parents to know that babies differ even at birth; the fact that a baby cries a lot does not necessarily mean that she or he is receiving the wrong kind of care.[17] Some are "easy," responding positively to new foods, people, and situations, and transmitting consistent cues (such as tired cry or hungry cry). Other infants are more "difficult." They have irregular sleeping or eating habits, adapt slowly to new situations, and may cry for extended periods for no apparent reason.[18]

Nevertheless, most of the parents I interviewed appeared happy to make what they saw as short-term sacrifices for long-term gain. Others weren't so sure. Andy said, "It's better than it used to be in some ways. But I don't know. I just feel like co-sleeping is part of an overall continuum of parenting that requires parents to sacrifice everything for uncertain benefits."

Although research and media attention have examined psychological depression and other distress among some pregnant and new mothers, fathers feel stress too.[19] Historically, fathers have been expected to be breadwinners and not necessarily competent in childcare. Today, however, our culture prescribes that "good" fathers not only assume considerable (generally primary) financial responsibility but also actively participate in the day-to-day aspects of parenting.[20] Mothers and many fathers are becoming more similar in the amount of time they spend and in the kinds of things they do with their children.[21] Nevertheless, mothers still assume primary responsibility for raising children. Employed or not, a mother is expected to be the child's primary *psychological parent*, assuming—with self-sacrifice when necessary—major emotional responsibility for her children's upbringing.[22]

Meanwhile, some studies show that women who are more pleased about their pregnancy are less likely later to view parenting as burdensome.[23] In fact, although many couples do, not all committed couples find the transition to parenthood to be especially difficult or upsetting to their relationship.[24] Nevertheless, becoming a parent typically involves what Roberta Coles calls the *paradox of parenting*: new parents feel overwhelmed, but the motivation to overcome their stress and do their best emanates from the stressor itself—the child as a source of love, joy, and satisfaction.[25]

In this chapter parents described their feelings and emotions about co-sleeping. The next chapter delves into another under-studied aspect of co-sleeping: how co-sleeping may influence parents' relationships and intimacy with their spouse or partner.

4

CO-SLEEPING, RELATIONSHIPS, AND INTIMACY

INTERVIEWER: How does co-sleeping influence intimacy with your spouse or partner, however you want to define that?

ANTHONY (married with one child age six months): It's not really conducive to "activities" in the bed. I suppose that it does maybe. I don't want to consider it a downside, but I think it has . . . it just complicates things. It's just . . . you have to think outside the box. I think it was our midwife who said, "Co-sleepers do it in the kitchen." They always say, "You know, there's other rooms in the house."

The above quotes illustrate what is one of Americans' major concerns about co-sleeping: that having children in the bed will disrupt the couple relationship and erode intimacy, especially sexual intimacy. Sex is among the most problematic areas of relationships for couples and is as important to relationship satisfaction as financial issues, spending time together, and expectations about how to allocate household tasks. Although I did not ask my study participants specifically about sex, most parents brought up both sexual and emotional intimacy with their spouse. For parents who were not married, I asked about their relationships with cohabiting partners, boyfriends, or girlfriends—whatever the case may be.

The worry that co-sleeping could negatively affect the couple relationship is not a trivial one. Marital satisfaction tends to be the highest in the first years of marriage and declines over time. As discussed in chapter 3, this decline is more rapid and dramatic for couples who make what sociologists refer to as "the transition to parenthood," which is the point at which couples have their first child. After this initial drop, marital satisfaction stabilizes during the childrearing years (albeit at a lower level), rebounds when the children leave the nest, but never returns to pre-child levels.[1] Thomas Bradbury and colleagues state that "children have the paradoxical effect of increasing the stability of the marriage while decreasing its quality."[2] Additional children are associated with further declines in marital satisfaction.

Given that most children born today are desired, planned, and welcomed by their parents, what accounts for the negative relationship between children and marital satisfaction? The addition of children to the household produces profound changes in the couple relationship.[3] First, there are the inevitable financial pressures associated with children: food, clothing, daycare, and the need to purchase a larger home. Second, the addition of children typically produces a significant alteration in the gender roles of husbands and wives.[4] Gender roles tend to be more similar and egalitarian in early marriage and among cohabiting and childless couples, including a more even distribution of housework and similarities in work hours and earnings. After the birth of a child, gender roles become more specialized and traditional. Employed mothers who have established fairly egalitarian relationships with their husbands may find their role becoming more traditional, particularly if they quit working to become full-time homemakers.[5] Whereas wives take on the majority of childrearing and domestic duties, husbands become more invested in their careers by, for example, working longer hours and trying for promotions. Mothers' work hours may become more irregular (such as working nights and weekends), which creates stress and adds to a couple's relationship conflict.[6] Finally and perhaps most importantly, couples with children spend more time taking care of their children's needs and less time taking care of their own. On the positive side, among parents who rated their relationship high in quality prior to becoming parents, the transition was easier, even with an unusually fussy baby.[7]

Very few studies have investigated the relationship between co-sleeping and marital satisfaction. One of the few is a Canadian study led by Rosemary Messmer, who studied eighty-one married mothers who shared a bed with their infant.[8] They found no relationship between time spent bedsharing and mothers' fatigue, sexual satisfaction, or satisfaction with bedsharing. Time spent bedsharing negatively affects their marital satisfaction, but only for *reactive* bedsharers, who are those who do not set out to bedshare but do so in response to disruptions in their child's sleep or their child's desire to co-sleep. Although not specific to co-sleeping, studies have found that sleep disruption, sleep loss, and infant crying are associated with lower marital satisfaction among new parents.[9] This can create a feedback loop, as relationship strain is associated with more troubled sleep.[10] However, existing studies are limited in that they focused on co-sleeping with infants and not older children. Nor were outcomes measured for fathers, single mothers, or ethnically diverse samples.

Although my research did not test causal relationships, the stories highlighted in this book—particularly in this chapter—shed light on how co-sleeping may affect couple relationship dynamics and intimacy. For example, Paul Rosenblatt found that the time couples spent together in the same bed at night has been found to be important in establishing and maintaining intimacy, through touching, snuggling, talking, and simply feeling each other's warmth.[11] Although he found that children could sometimes interfere, he did not examine co-sleeping per se.

Creating Closeness

Many parents felt that co-sleeping brought them and their family closer as a family. For some couples, co-sleeping enhanced family cohesion, defined as "the emotional bonding that couples and family members have toward one another."[12] Allison, who is married and has three children, explained:

> INTERVIEWER: If you were asked to describe how you feel about co-sleeping what would you say? Is this a good thing? A bad thing?
>
> ALLISON: For us, it's a comfortable thing because our family is pretty close. We do most things together generally, so this is kind of an extension of that.

Similarly, when I asked about what co-sleeping is like for Charlie, who is married with a three-year-old son, he replied, "I think it's kind of neat. Since our son sleeps right in between us, I've got to say it does feel comforting and there's a closeness in the family when his arm is up against mine. I think, 'Okay, that's nice; okay, cool.' I feel safe and secure, too, I guess."

A number of parents said that co-sleeping enhanced rather than detracted from their relationship with their partner. When asked about this, Mandy responded,

> I would probably say it enhances it because I think that the way we work together is by cooperation. Very few decisions in our house are unilateral. Having the agreement, whatever the issue is, strengthens our relationship and we're very aware of that. And that's kind of a big thing in our family. We also think it's good for the children to see us on the same page, and we're

also very aware of that. So we rarely ever express disagreement in front of the children.

Several of the fathers in the study expressed this same sentiment. Anthony is married and has a six-month-old son. When asked about whether co-sleeping matters to closeness and intimacy with his wife, he said,

> For me, I think it makes me love her and more bonded to her and we like how amazing and natural it is for our son to sleep with us. Just how my wife's so attached to him and how well he's doing, and just seeing them together. In the morning sometimes I'm getting dressed and they're still asleep. It's just nice to see him just so content. I think it's just a beautiful thing to see.

Creating Distance

Co-sleeping could also interfere with a couple's ability to maintain emotional intimacy. Having children in the bed presented a particular challenge to couples who had always equated nighttime with "couple time," especially for couples who had been more focused on the romantic quality of their relationship.[13]

Jody, married with three kids, ages eight, six, and one-and-a-half, said, "For us as a couple, we've always tried to keep it that our bedroom is very sacred and that we don't want the kids getting comfortable with it. We've always talked to them in terms of, 'you sleep in your room. This is your bed. This is where you stay,' because we don't have a lot of time together. So as much as we can we want to keep our bedroom our bedroom." Janessa and her husband sleep in different rooms of the house. When asked if she and her husband miss sleeping together she said, "Well, yes. I think the wife and husband should sleep together. You can talk about a lot of things. It's just like now there's no time to talk. Yes,

I miss that feeling. Maybe this summer I will try to train [my son]. Train him to sleep alone with his brother."

Many parents expressed frustration over simply having time alone with their spouse. Whereas Mandy (mentioned above) expressed how co-sleeping enhanced their closeness, Brad pointed out that co-sleeping is not without its downsides. He said,

> [We are missing] all those different benefits that come along with the kids sleeping through the night and us sleeping together. Even stuff like being able to stay up and watch a movie, you know? You can't do that when there's a child getting out of her bed. You have to go in and comfort them and lay with them for twenty minutes. It's impossible to, "Oh, we got five minutes into the movie and should we pick it back up now or not? By that point you're like f— that. I'm going to bed. I'm tired."

Communication and Conflict

As described above, co-sleeping can bring couples closer but also create distance. In general, the "separate spheres" for men and women associated with the early years of childrearing may contribute to increased conflict and lack of understanding between partners. In an eight-year longitudinal study of 218 couples, both husbands and wives reported a sudden drop in the quality of their communication, ability to manage conflict, and relationship satisfaction after their first child was born.[14] For decades, John Gottman from the University of Washington has been studying how couple communication affects relationship quality. His findings indicate that how well couples communicate is a strong and consistent predictor of subsequent divorce. Whereas warmth, cohesion, and supportive communication is positively associated with child and adult well-being and family stability, he found that poor communication is strongly negatively associated with marital quality. Once children are in the picture, the quality of communication becomes even more central to marital happiness.[15]

The quality of communication mattered greatly with respect to how well the couples in my study adjusted to co-sleeping with their children, especially for couples who had differing opinions about the children's being in the bed—importantly, because unresolved and/or ongoing conflict negatively affects the well-being of both children and adults and reduces marital happiness.[16] More often than not the father did not want to co-sleep. When asked about whether they planned on co-sleeping should they have another child, Kaylee, who has a three-year-old son, and who is cohabiting with her son's father said,

> We have talked about that because of the fact that we're going to be getting married and we want another kid. We have talked about the situation with our son still sleeping with us and that we cannot allow that to happen with the second one. Now, I can't say that's not going to happen. I mean when you're tired and you've been up all night, you just do whatever you do to get some sleep. I can say I'm going to try not to let it happen with the next child. Like I told [my partner], I can't make any promises because another part of it is that he is still trying to understand. I said, "You have to almost put yourself in my shoes. You would have done the same thing." He's kind of just begun to understand that truthfully. It took him a long time to understand that because he was really not happy with the sleeping situation and he blames me for starting it. I said, "Well, if you were there when he was screaming all night I think you'd understand."

Couples have many different styles of communication, though. All of these can be effective at handling conflict as long as partners have similar styles. For example, in Gottman's research some couples handled conflict by "agreeing to disagree."[17] A number of the parents in my study had adopted that approach, perhaps because talking about co-sleeping implies taking action, which many couples weren't ready to do. When I asked Gina whether she and her wife ever planned to sit down and talk about the situation, she said,

> You know, probably not. Probably out of cowardice on my part. I think she has a lot of good reasons for wanting us to kind of buckle down on the kids, and help them figure their own way out. I can't even disagree with all of them except it feels like so much the right thing to be doing. It's just so comforting, and "lovely" is just the word that I keep coming back to. I know that that's not everybody's experience. It's not necessarily [my partner's] experience. She doesn't necessarily like to have them wrap themselves around your arm all night. So no, if we talked about it, we would have to come up with a plan and do something, and who wants to do that?

Other parents had more or less "surrendered" to co-sleeping. Becky's husband did not want their two children, ages three and six, in the bed. She said, "[My husband] was very opposed to my sleeping with her from the beginning, but he has kind of just given up because he sees that we're all getting sleep. I don't know that he necessarily agrees or approves of it, but he doesn't say anything about it anymore. It's not like it's an issue. I don't feel that it is at this point."

Sexual Intimacy

Numerous studies have found that sexual satisfaction is important to relationship happiness and frequency of sexual activity is highly correlated with marital satisfaction.[18] It is well-known that most couples have less sex after the birth of a child because the needs of the new baby take precedence over the needs of the couple.[19] This reduced emphasis on sexual intimacy can extend into the child's school-age years and beyond. For example, in a longitudinal study of 258 parents, both mothers and fathers reported a significant decline in sensuality (hugging, kissing, cuddling), sexual frequency, and contentment when their child was between six months and eight years old.[20] In another study of 169 first-time parents', "role overload" (when the demands placed on a person are greater than their ability to handle them) at six months post-birth was associated with reduced sexual satisfaction among both mothers and fathers twelve months later.[21]

To my knowledge, only one study has specifically investigated the relationship between co-sleeping and sexual satisfaction—that of Messmer and colleagues, who found no relationship between bedsharing and the sexual satisfaction of new mothers. In Rosenblatt's study of couples, he wrote that "quite a few" parents expressed concerns about their children hearing them having intercourse and felt it was difficult to have intercourse "freely, frequently, and spontaneously."[22] This was true even though the children were sleeping in a different room. What is it like, then, for parents whose children sleep in the same bed?

Dr. Calvin Colarusso, in a letter appearing in *The Journal of Pediatrics*, argued that co-sleeping should not be practiced because it interferes with the "resumption and elaboration of parental sexuality and intimacy." He claimed, "A third person in the sexual bed is at least a distraction and always a competitor for the concern, attention, and affection of one or both sexual partners." However, in the same volume, Dr. Nancy Powers argued that if a child is in the bed, parents will "no doubt create other opportunities for sexual activity that do not directly expose the child to such activity," such as putting the child in his or her own bed for part of the night.[23] Similarly, parenting guru Dr. William Sears encourages couples to be creative with respect to making time for sex. In their in-depth interviews with ten first-time parents, researchers found that new parents often compensated for a reduction in sexual activity by expressing reciprocal tenderness toward one another, caressing each other, and by setting aside "alone time" that may include sex.[24]

Many parents in my study indeed found alternatives to having sex at night in the bed or, as Wendy stated, they "work around it." Charlie's wife Gabby said that co-sleeping with their son affects their ability to be sexually intimate "most of the time," which she said is "a little frustrating," but that they "figure out other ways" like going in the TV room once their son falls asleep. Charlie agreed and said, "you have to get creative because you can't just do it spur of the moment. You have to maybe close the door or run downstairs."

Karen and Andy have two boys, age four and two. When asked about having time together, they said,

ANDY: It's not really happening. [*laughs*] We hire babysitters. To have a relationship.

INTERVIEWER: Do you have "date night" or something like that?

KAREN: Our date night is our basement. We have an entire basement down there that's like another apartment. You can lock the door and . . .

ANDY: We just lock ourselves in our basement.

KAREN: Or we have to beg and plead one of our mothers to come watch the children.

ANDY: It's hard. I don't know.

Other parents did not feel that co-sleeping was a barrier to sex. Ingrid and Victor have two daughters, ages three and six months.

INTERVIEWER: What about you guys and your relationship?

INGRID: I think one of my biggest annoyances when people talk about co-sleeping is they think that we don't ever have sex.

INTERVIEWER: Is that a stereotype sometimes?

INGRID: Yes! And I always tell people "our kids go to bed before us." With [our older daughter] it's been a lot harder because sometimes she'll go to sleep and she'll be fine and then sometimes she'll go to sleep and she'll be up until I go to bed.

INTERVIEWER: Do you have time together?

INGRID: Yes. There's two hours and a whole other house that we can spend time in. I think the co-sleeping hasn't really hindered it. I think it's just . . .

VICTOR: With two children. I mean we're a lot busier.

INGRID: Yeah. Especially when you're working late at night and some nights I don't want to stay up and wait until you get home, I just want to go to sleep, you know? So I think that's true even if they were sleeping in their bed, don't you? That it would be the same?

VICTOR: Probably.

INGRID: So I don't think it's hindering anything. I think like our whole family relationship is closer just because we wake up in the morning and our kids wake up the same time we do and we always just like to lie in bed.

Although Victor seemed a bit more tentative in saying that the children don't hinder their sex life, both of them were in general agreement that co-sleeping does not necessarily limit sexual intimacy.

Although not always viewed as a significant problem in the relationship, co-sleeping could present a challenge. Chris is an older father in his second marriage. His story was typical. When I asked him if he and his wife ever discussed the matter, he said,

> We definitely have had discussions about it. There are times where we say we want to get back to a normal sleeping pattern. There is no doubt that it's affected our intimacy. Not to the point that it's jeopardizing our relationship but . . .

> INTERVIEWER: Do you guys figure out other strategies?

> CHRIS: You know, we talk about it, but that's about as far as it goes. [laughs] I guess it's an open discussion. Prior to having our son, we were a very active couple, so it's definitely been a change for us. It hasn't affected our desire to be together, but certainly that's probably one of the driving discussions or issues related to getting him into his own bed.

For the last year, Kaylee's three-year-old son has been sleeping with her while her fiancé (her son's dad) sleeps in the playroom. She wants her son to move back into his own room, but she says they haven't been strict about it. With respect to her fiancé, she said,

> It's going okay. I will say it takes a toll on the relationship. Because of the fact that we don't get any time to ourselves because he's in the middle of us all the time. And that's totally fine but I think it's more of an issue because it's hard. We don't really get to see each other a whole lot during the week and then our weekends are kind of supposed to be our time. We get a lot of family time and we usually try to go do stuff, but then when it comes to being together—like even being like affectionate, like cuddling, anything like that—he doesn't let it happen. He's very much, "My mommy, my mommy." Like even if [my fiancé] kisses me, he's got to come give me a

kiss. "Those are my kisses!" But I've probably created that because if I was very stern about his going and sleeping in his bed, I'm sure that we could do it. So I kind of almost blame myself when it comes down to it, but it is what it is.

When I asked her what she thought her fiancé might say about it, she replied,

Well, he's a guy, so he would probably say that he's not getting enough attention, sexually, from me. But you know, there's just no time. There really isn't and that's horrible to say but it's like if you want me to be strictly honest, there just isn't. I mean we're young, you know? Like this is the time where we should be more loving toward each other I guess is the clean way of putting it. But I mean we just don't get a lot of that time. We need it. We need to do it—set a time for us and get him out of our bed so we have that time, because that's like the only time that we would get—but it just hasn't happened.

Fathers, Partners, and Boyfriends

In previous research, concern over how co-sleeping affects sexual intimacy has focused primarily on fathers. For all couples, whether co-sleeping or not, mothers may experience significant physical and hormonal changes after the birth of a child, resulting in a low libido, vaginal dryness, negative body image, breast pain, and complications and physical trauma from childbirth.[25] In his book *Becoming a Father*, William Sears devotes an entire chapter to sex after childbirth. He describes how in his experience, mothers "in their hearts" feel sleeping with their baby is the right thing to do but they often don't because of pressure from husbands. Dr. Sears states, "a tired mother becomes a tired wife and the whole family suffers."[26] Other research has found that many new fathers are unhappy with the reduced sexual attention and frequency of intercourse with their wife, and so on. In one study of 131 new parents, fathers, more so than mothers, thought that the quality of the couple's sex life declined with a general deterioration of the relationship.[27] Other work suggests that fathers may feel abandoned or jealous of the time the wife is spending with the baby.[28] Tracy and Jake have two young boys. She said,

> Yeah, you know, I just need my bubble. I need a little space for a little while. Jake and I had some issues with that because he would want attention from me, not just physical attention, but I'm just spent. You are going to have to take care of yourself because I don't want to talk to anybody. I don't want you touching me. I don't want to be near anybody. So I think that was probably the biggest disadvantage.

Matthew and Jody have three children, ages eight, six, and seventeen months. I asked Matthew about how co-sleeping affects his relationship with his wife.

MATTHEW: I can see where you could have some dads, husbands, males who in our situation, especially if it had been our first and we were going through this for several months—not several months, but definitely an extended period of time—where the physical aspect of a husband and wife's relationship could just drive a guy nuts. I mean in all honesty, I think it could. So with that being said I think if you don't have kind of a team effort of support there, it could get pretty negative pretty quickly.

INTERVIEWER: In terms of your relationship with your partner?

MATTHEW: Well yeah. I think very quickly we become selfish individuals and we're, like, well . . . we've been taking care of the child for five nights in a row, how about taking care of me? That type of thing. So I wouldn't be surprised if you find some of that. We've kind of developed an awareness of the kind of time frame we're talking about here to get through it. I can see where that part right there could become pretty stressful for a couple. I said before: finding a really good therapist can give you some hope.

INTERVIEWER: Tell me a little bit more about how you've gotten yourself through that particularly difficult time and come out on the other side okay as a couple.

MATTHEW: As a couple, I think there's different kind of categories that have to be satisfied and fulfilled. I think one is you have to be talking to each other because I think it's very easy, if on a night my wife hasn't slept and at 5:30 a.m. she's bringing me [my son] and I've got to entertain him for an hour while she sleeps and I'm trying to get ready for work and maybe we both work. That in and of itself can just make you be at each other's throats so quickly if you're not talking stuff out. I mean if you can't send a text during the day like, "Hey, how are you doing, how are the kids doing?" or an e-mail to let each other know that you're still there for each other, you're still thinking about each other, you're still praying for each other, whatever it is. You have to be talking to each other and figuring out how to meet each other's needs so you don't become the stereotypical dad. You have to find a way to meet the emotional and physical needs that as human beings you have.

Jody, Matthew's wife, continued.

JODY: I would say that he found it extremely frustrating, because there's literally no time for us and all of my time and all of my focus is kids, kids, kids, kids, kids. And that really puts a strain on the marriage relationship because how do you have physical intimacy when you have a kid plopped in the middle of the bed? Even though the spouse is supposed to have some understanding of, like, the child needs you, there's still a massive level of frustration. It's still, like, can't we just sleep and be by ourselves and be a married couple?

INTERVIEWER: Tell me a little about how you found ways to work through that and maintain a marital relationship.

JODY: It was a constant back and forth of a level of understanding where we're on an even playing field. Do either of us like it? No. This isn't necessarily going to pacify where he was. I feel like one of the strengths of us working through so much is communication. Talking things through, like, I'm very angry right now, this is ridiculous, this shouldn't be going on. And even though I'm not saying you're right, it's fine. It's the fact that to be able to talk it out kind of gives voice to what's going on, but it doesn't necessarily change the situation.

INTERVIEWER: So communication . . .

JODY: Communication is huge.

Similarly, Paul explained whether co-sleeping affected intimacy with his wife.

PAUL: Like I said, I do enjoy having him sleep in the bed. It makes it harder for me and [my wife] to be in the same bed together though, you know? I used to spoon or cuddle her or whatever you want to call it and we don't do that anymore.

INTERVIEWER : That's a drawback?

PAUL: Yes. That's a definite drawback. But like I said I do enjoy having him there.

INTERVIEWER: Are there any other drawbacks that you can think of?

PAUL: Well, obviously, what goes along with that is that our sex life isn't much at all. [*laughs*]

INTERVIEWER: So you don't really get alone time together?

PAUL: No. No. We don't.

INTERVIEWER: How do you feel about that?

PAUL: It's a strain on us for sure. It's hard but I enjoy the *family* time we have together, you know? But me and her, we really don't. That's a definite drawback—to not have your own space together.

For other husbands, however, co-sleeping did not seem to be an important factor with respect to their sexual satisfaction. As described above, many fathers prioritized "family time" over sex, at least temporarily. Bruce is married and has a three-year-old daughter. When asked about whether co-sleeping affects his intimacy with his wife, he said, "No, because at night we are both just smoked. So, our intimate moments happen in the morning, in the afternoon, or something like that. If [my daughter] takes a nap, we're, like, 'Hey, why don't we take a nap (wink, wink)?' So we're fine."

What about parents with boyfriends who sleep over? Sarah is a single mom with a six-year-old girl and three-year-old boy. I asked her whether co-sleeping has ever been an issue in a relationship.

INTERVIEWER: What if you want to have someone stay overnight?

SARAH: It's come into play. Once before. It was so funny. The person spending the night was like plastered up—hugging the wall, if that's even possible. That's one of those nights when I was up the entire night just trying to get [my son] back to his bed.

INTERVIEWER: It didn't faze [your son] to be in the middle of you two?

SARAH: Oh, no he doesn't care! [*laughs*]

INTERVIEWER: What about the person in the bed? Did that person say anything?

SARAH: It was probably weird. I don't know. The person didn't have any kids. But I don't think he could have possibly gotten any closer to the wall.

CONCLUSION

Co-sleeping is worrisome to many people because it is thought that having children in the bed is disruptive to the couple relationship. Specifically, co-sleeping is thought to present a challenge to couples' sexual relationship because the bed is still considered the primary location for sex. In *Two in a Bed*, Rosenblatt found that for many couples, "sexual intercourse was a regular part of their going-to-sleep routine."[29] Another common concern is that the child would be exposed to "improper sexual relations."[30]

The transition to parenthood is stressful for all couples, and most couples put their children's needs above their own. This was the case for all of the parents in my study. Granted, this may be a particularly committed group of parents considering that they co-sleep with their children. My interviews indicate that co-sleeping can either enhance or detract from couple closeness, and for most couples, there were elements of both. Communication was a central part of navigating conflict between partners, although conflict could be handled as much through talking as *not talking*.

The parents in my study were generally open to talking about sex and brought the issue up themselves. These discussions could sometimes cause discomfort, exemplified by long pauses, stops and starts of sentences and nervous laughter, and so forth. Oftentimes any embarrassment with talking about sex on the part of parents (mostly fathers) was handled through humor and euphemistic descriptions.

I did not find strong evidence that fathers were particularly jealous of the time their wives spent with their child or were upset that sex was not as frequent. Although a number of fathers discussed their frustration with not having sex, these feelings were not exclusive to men. Most parents, both fathers and mothers, viewed the situation as temporary and overall were optimistic that they would return to their previous patterns. Contrary to the conventional wisdom, finding time for sex was not always a problem for couples and the majority found other ways to be sexually intimate. More recent generations of men and women, products of the sexual revolution, tend to have more liberal attitudes about the time and place for sex (i.e., it is no longer restricted to the marital bed at night).

On the one hand, I did not find compelling evidence that co-sleeping itself was a strong determinant of marital satisfaction. I could find no patterns in attitudes or experiences by race, ethnicity, education, income, family structure, or any of the other variables examined. Although parents said that co-sleeping could present challenges to intimacy, these were not viewed as long-term problems. On the other hand, simply the rigors of parenting young children translated into less time spent for couples to relax and spend time together, and for several couples, appeared to negatively affect their emotional and sexual relationship. Social support from others—family members, friends, coworkers, and so forth—can make all the difference to parents of young children whether the family co-sleeps or not. Parenting is less stressful when a mother's expectations are met concerning how much support she will receive, including how much her partner will be involved with the baby.[31] The next chapter examines just that—the amount of social support that co-sleeping couples receive or do not receive—and the implications of this for their relationships and their own well-being.

5

OPENNESS, SECRECY, AND REACTIONS FROM OTHERS

JANET (married with three children ages five, three, and one): I was actually working for a children's hospital at that time and one of their big things was "co-sleeping is bad," you know? Putting the baby on their back to sleep, never sleeping with your baby, never having your baby in the bed with you. That was really drilled into me and prior to becoming a parent, I was very hard core on, "This is the rule, and you never sleep with a baby. Do you want to kill your baby?"

As noted in chapter 1, although co-sleeping is widely accepted around the world, it remains controversial in the United States. Critics of co-sleeping are primarily concerned with its safety, a view generally supported by physicians and the broader medical community, arguably one of our most revered and influential social institutions. Others voice concerns that co-sleeping reduces the quality of parents' and children's sleep, that co-sleeping may lead to social and emotional problems in children, and, as discussed in the previous chapter, that co-sleeping erodes intimacy between parents. Co-sleeping advocates maintain that the benefits of co-sleeping far outweigh the risks.

However, parents who co-sleep with their children are engaging in a practice the general public deems unacceptable. In the United States, ideas about family life are more conservative relative to other industrialized countries. Americans have strong opinions as to how children should be raised and generally do not hesitate to voice those opinions, especially with the rise in social media and the anonymity it provides. Through the use of Facebook, Instagram, Twitter, and other venues, parenting is more and more likely to be conducted in a "public" setting. The downside to all this sharing however, is that parents and their decisions are increasingly scrutinized by others. Stories of "mom shaming" abound. One mom-blogger was told she should "kill herself" after writing what was meant to be a humorous take on parenting's negative side.[1]

As described in previous chapters, modern parents are experiencing a high level of stress as they juggle work and family roles. Moreover, what constitutes a "good" parent has changed. Parenting in the individualistic and competitive culture of the United States in the context of poor institutional supports for families only compounds these pressures. Under such conditions, having a supportive social network could mean the difference between a confident, self-assured parent and an insecure, wavering one.[2] It is therefore important to examine co-sleeping parents' social resources and support.

The quality of parents' support networks matter. For example, involvement in a religious community has been shown to reduce the decline in marital satisfaction that comes with a new child.[3] Among working mothers with young children, coworkers can be a vital source of support.[4] The focus of this chapter is how parents who co-sleep with their children navigate social relationships within a cultural context largely disapproving of this practice. In this chapter, parents describe their level of comfort discussing their sleeping arrangements with different audiences, such as the children's pediatrician, extended family members, and friends. This chapter includes parents' descriptions of reactions they have received from others upon telling them that they were co-sleeping with their children.

COMFORT LEVEL WITH DISCUSSING CO-SLEEPING

All the parents I interviewed were aware co-sleeping is controversial and expressed varying degrees of comfort with respect to telling others they were co-sleeping. Among parents deeply committed to attachment parenting or who were generally confident with respect to their approach, co-sleeping was either a "non-issue" or they simply ignored negative remarks. (All the parents in my study reported receiving negative remarks.) Most of these parents were embedded in social networks supportive of co-sleeping—that is, "birds of a feather flock together." These parents discussed co-sleeping along with other topics related to their children. In general, however, whether and how co-sleeping was discussed was dependent upon the audience and parents' perception of how they thought the information would be received. As one couple said, "We finally told our parents that we were co-sleeping." Many parents, anticipating a negative reaction, hid that they co-slept or "lied by omission," or otherwise didn't volunteer the information. Other parents explained how they were "found out." These themes can be seen below, which describes parents' comfort level with discussing co-sleeping with various members of their social network and what they said (or did not say).

Doctors and Medical Practitioners

Janet's interview above reflects the medical community's prevailing negative attitude toward co-sleeping. Anticipating a negative reaction from her children's pediatrician, Allison, a married mother with three children (ages twelve, nine, and six), didn't mention to him that they were co-sleeping.

INTERVIEWER: So you have had conversations where people expressed a little bit of concern?

ALLISON: Right, concern. But I will tell you that I did not tell my pediatrician, just because I did not want to get the . . . because he is not a Sears follower . . . I did not want to get "the talk."

Evelyn has a fifteen-month-old son and cohabits with her child's father. Like Allison, she did not tell her child's pediatrician that their baby slept with them. She said, "Every time we'd go to the pediatrician and he kept on telling us, 'Sleep on his back, on a flat surface, on a crib.' I just went along with it. I never told him that [our child] was co-sleeping with us just because I was scared of being summoned or something about him, you know?"

Some parents specifically chose a pro-co-sleeping doctor to avoid these kinds of responses. These parents were committed to attachment parenting and desired a practitioner supportive of co-sleeping and other alternatives to conventional medical care. For example, some of the parents I interviewed were advocates of home birth, prolonged breastfeeding, and flexibility with respect to the timing and necessity of immunizations. Danielle, for example, said she interviewed "tons" of pediatricians, after being told repeatedly that co-sleeping wasn't safe. "Every time we went to a doctor's appointment she asked, 'How's the baby sleeping?' I'd just say, 'Fine; she's sleeping in her own bed,' cause every time we get the same lecture about how it's not safe." After finding her first doctor was not supportive of co-sleeping, Sandra, "changed pediatricians when he was a month old. He went to one appointment there and then we switched. And the new pediatrician is very open-minded, and he has an opinion but he will not share it with you just because what you do is OK with him." Crystal's doctor, after initially recommending co-sleeping, told her that she "needed to start letting her [her two-year-old daughter] cry it out." She, too, found a new doctor.

Family Members

Janet and her husband did not initially disclose to anyone that they co-slept with their children but did so after they had their third child.

> INTERVIEWER: Let's talk about your parents and your husband's parents.

> JANET: Yes. I have a different perspective because both of my parents are medical professionals so not only do I get the parent pressure of "don't sleep with your children." I also get the medical professional pressure because my dad's a pharmacist and my mom is a nurse practitioner. And so as medical professionals they teach people: don't sleep with your children, you could kill your child that way. So I don't think we admitted to co-sleeping with them until probably when my [last child] was born. I don't know that they ever knew that we co-slept with Max, my oldest.

Gina is married and has two children, ages six and three. She discusses how comfortable she is talking with her family about co-sleeping. Unlike Janet, she was very open about it.

> INTERVIEWER: So have you talked to your extended families about how your kids sleep with you?

> GINA: We talk a lot about it. We talk about it when I'm frustrated about it. If I'm sort of like, "Oh we haven't had any personal time at all!" That sort of thing. Everybody knows that they sleep with us.

INTERVIEWER: And no one bats an eye?

GINA: No, and my mother says—and this is her response to most parenting problems—"You are the solution, [Gina]."

The following comes from Sharon, who is a divorced, single mother of a thirteen-year-old daughter. She told her family she co-sleeps even though she knew they'd disapprove.

INTERVIEWER: Were your parents aware that you co-slept with your daughter? Is this something you talked about with them?

SHARON: Ugh, yeah. I don't think they were extremely impressed. I think they felt like I coddled her, because they were staying here one time when I would have to go up and put her down and they were, like, eye rolling kind of. Like she was being babied like that. Like she wouldn't just go to sleep.

INTERVIEWER: Did they ever know how often you guys slept in the same bed every night?

SHARON: I don't know. I don't think so. It wasn't something we really talked about. They knew that I had to help her get to sleep.

INTERVIEWER: How comfortable would you be telling them that you guys slept together in the same bed every night for five years?

SHARON: I'd be fine. I don't mind telling them.

INTERVIEWER: What would their reaction be?

SHARON: At this point probably disinterest because they're so egomaniacal in their old age. If I had to project their opinions,

I don't think they'd particularly approve, but they've learned not to intervene.

INTERVIEWER: Ok, these are your parents. What about your sister?

SHARON: She does not approve either. She just would feel like, you know, another coddling mechanism. But she has no children. But she knows everything about everything. [*laughs*]

Sandra, who has a one-year-old son, said that, with respect to her family, "It's pretty much 'don't ask, don't tell.'" Alice said, "They ask about how she is sleeping and I just say, 'oh, good,' and don't really say much more because most of the time they don't approve. With doctors, she said they think it's "not the best, but I just say, 'Okay, thanks for the advice,' and I'll smile and go on with my day." Laura has a six-month-old daughter. Although she said she's, "comfortable with everything I've done to this point and the decisions I've made," she said her sister made her feel judged, like she was doing something "odd" or "strange." Such criticism may lead even the most confident parents to question their choices.

Friends and Others

Victor and Ingrid have two daughters, ages three and six months. He described the reaction he anticipated his friends would have if he ever disclosed he co-slept with his children.

INTERVIEWER: What about any friends of yours? Is this something you know about from your friends or talking with other guys? Would this be something you'd share?

VICTOR: I would share it for sure but I don't, I guess, when I'm around my friends, and a lot of my friends don't have children.

Even if my friends do have children, I mean it's not something we talk about. I mean, the wives, they'd sit at the table or sit on the couch and talk about that kind of stuff. We wouldn't talk about it. Like, "What are your sleeping arrangements with your child?" [*laughs*]

INTERVIEWER: If you said, "Hey guys, I co-sleep with my daughters . . ."

VICTOR: I don't think they would care, they'd be like, "Why are you even talking about it?"

Anthony and Samantha have a three-month-old son. Concerned about SIDS, they had done a lot of research on co-sleeping and how to bedshare safely.

ANTHONY: I feel like sometimes with the bedsharing thing we haven't necessarily really, like, gone into a lot of detail with certain people.

SAMANTHA: Yeah. We just say he sleeps in our room with us. We don't . . .

ANTHONY: Yeah, because some . . .

SAMANTHA: Certain groups of people.

ANTHONY: Certain people we don't talk about it with. And it's not that we're ashamed or afraid of it, it's just that it could kind of lead into more of a conversation.

SAMANTHA: You know, when I was pregnant I had someone at work tell me, "I know so-and-so, and who slept with their baby and they rolled over and killed them." And I was like, "I'm like seven months pregnant and you're telling me this? Why would you say that to a pregnant woman?" It's just, you kind of get that unsolicited advice when you open yourself up to certain people.

ANTHONY: I think we're a pretty good judge of who would be interested and who would just provide weird feedback. So, yeah I think a lot of people ask, "Is he sleeping in his crib well?" And I'm like, "Well, he's still in our room for now." That sort of thing.

Married couple Diana and Paul have two boys, one of whom is eight months old. While Diana initially was hesitant about telling people she and her husband co-slept with their children, she became more confident about it. She said this:

DIANA: I've gotten to the point where I just really don't care what people think. I mean, if they ask I will tell them.

INTERVIEWER: It sounds like it wasn't always that way. What are some circumstances when it wasn't really comfortable to talk about?

DIANA: When they would say, "Well that's why! You're having your child sleep with you. That's why you're not getting any sleep! That's why he's not on a sleep pattern."

INTERVIEWER: Who would say that?

DIANA: I would say coworkers. Not really family. Friends, you know; acquaintances, I guess. Just different people.

INTERVIEWER: If people ask, you'll tell them about your family's sleeping arrangements but it sounds like you don't just volunteer the information in conversation.

DIANA: No, I would volunteer it.

INTERVIEWER: So, you would bring it up that co-sleeping works well in your family?

DIANA: Yeah. And I love it. In fact, I've actually told people I wouldn't trade it.

INTERVIEWER: Would you recommend it to people?

DIANA: Yes!

Carley is a married mother with two boys, ages four and six. She describes the circumstances under which she tells others about sometimes co-sleeping with her children.

INTERVIEWER: Is co-sleeping something your family is aware of? Have you gotten advice?

CARLEY: Sometimes I talk to other people. I'm pretty open with everyone in terms of, "Oh, you know my kids have been in my bed again." You know, where I'm frustrated because my kids have been in my bed or I have had to sleep with them. When I ask people, "What's your situation like?" or "When did your kids leave you alone?" That sort of thing.

Janet explained how she and her husband used "doorknob covers" to keep their children from coming into their room.

INTERVIEWER: I have never heard of that. Why do you do that?

JANET: Because we don't want them wandering around at night. We don't want them playing around in the bathroom and things like that. We don't have a doorknob cover on our boys' room because [our younger son] can't get out of his crib and my oldest can open a door with a door knob cover on anyway. It's more for when they are younger than five, like my daughter. She has a door knob cover on her room because we don't want her wandering around in the middle of the night because she is such a social person. She likes to be in close physical proximity to our family members. So if she were to wake up in the middle of the night she would come into our bedroom and try to crawl into bed with us or go crawl into bed with [our older son]. He is actually a very hard sleeper and so he will sleep through any noise, but if you physically get on him and touch him and shake him, he will wake up. So she'd climb in there and get on him and stroke his face and just talk to him and touch him and then of course he would wake up. So that's why we lock her in. I don't tell very many people we do that. [*laughs*]

I then asked what happens when her daughter gets up and she wants to get out but can't. Janet said she does that pretty much every night. Her daughter will get up and stand by the door and yell, "I have a pee, I have a pee" and so Janet goes and lets her out.

Spouses

I was surprised to find that some parents (in all cases mothers) kept the fact that they co-slept from their husband. Renee is married and has three young boys. She is a proponent of co-sleeping but he was less inclined to let the children into the bed. She said, "My middle one, he is six, gets very emotional and has nightmares. He came because he said he was being 'pursued by beasts.' So he's like, 'Why can't we ever sleep with you guys?' And I said, because I'm the only one here, and Papa is not here, 'sure come and snuggle in.' So he slept in there and I'm like, 'it's gonna be our little secret.'"

Renee's story provides an example of how culture affects co-sleeping. Living in the United States, she said,

All the comments I heard while here were more negative than positive, such as, "you've got to teach the kid to sleep in his own bed." Whereas if I were talking to someone from my family it's like it's the most natural thing in the world. So that's why I thought it was more cultural. I don't feel as much hostility, I guess, from the people I know. But then again, most of them are foreigners. Not Latin, but foreigners.

REACTIONS RECEIVED TO CO-SLEEPING

Some parents do not disclose to anyone that they are co-sleeping or disclose this information to some audiences but not others. The following section describes some of the various reactions the parents received when they have mentioned it.

The Medical Community

Doctors and nurses unsupportive of co-sleeping mentioned both medical and nonmedical reasons to not co-sleep. Janessa, who grew up in China, slept with her sisters and their mom and said that it was "a good experience." Her sister, who still lives in China, sleeps with her own daughter. Janessa said, "In America, the doctor said, 'you need to put him in his own bedroom, in his own bed.' The thing is, it's hard to separate now because he doesn't want to sleep alone."

Mandy's daughter has sleep problems, including "night terrors." As a result, she and her husband began bringing her into their bed.

INTERVIEWER: Has anyone ever given you unsolicited advice on how to put your kids to bed?

MANDY: We went to see the doctor because my daughter was having a whole lot of trouble sleeping. So we went to a physician, and she actually said to my daughter, "The rule is, children sleep in the children's bed, and parents sleep in the parents' bed."

INTERVIEWER: Really?

MANDY: Yes, she was adamant that that should not happen. That that was a parenting mistake you would never get around. You know, we appreciate that feedback. And sometimes when we're trying to get our daughter out of our bed, we'll say, "children sleep in the children's bed." Because she knows it, right? It was so impactful for her.

Sarah is a divorced, single mother with two children, ages six and three. She describes her pediatrician's reaction:

SARAH: The only person who's given me some backlash is my son's doctor. My pediatrician asked about it and I said, "No, he sleeps pretty much with me every night, but starts in his own bed and just runs in in the middle of the night." And she's like, "Well, you should start by putting a blanket down on the floor." And I'm like, "Okay, that's not gonna work."

INTERVIEWER: Did she talk about a justification for why she suggested he not be there with you?

SARAH: No, that's all she said. She was just like, "You need to start training him not to do that." And gave me a couple of ideas.

INTERVIEWER: But you weren't seeking advice?

SARAH: No. I've heard different doctors have different opinions. People have told me, "My doctor said do whatever works." While other doctors have said, "You really don't want to start going down that road" kind of thing. And see, I don't see what the problem is. I don't think I'm raising weird kids or anything like that. I just . . . I don't know. I had one conversation with my mom when she asked me to have my daughter cry it out, I was like, "No way. I'm waaay too uncomfortable with this." And that's when I did research on co-sleeping, crying it out, all that stuff.

Ingrid and Victor had talked to her pediatrician and chiropractor about her child's sleep patterns. They received rather mixed messages about it.

INTERVIEWER: When the babies were little, did your pediatrician have anything to say about co-sleeping?

INGRID: No. Our pediatrician did say that [the baby] should only be getting up a couple times in the night to nurse. And she said to try not to nurse her in the middle of the night—maybe like one time. But she's never talked about co-sleeping versus not co-sleeping. She said that if that's what you prefer that's fine. She never has anything bad to say about it. Our chiropractor is very pro co-sleeping, which is kind of funny.

Midwives tend to have accepting attitudes toward co-sleeping and most actively promote it, which was the case for Karen and Andy. Andy said, "Within our circle, it's very accepted even expected, that you're going to co-sleep. Our midwife was very encouraging. The pediatrician we first saw was very opposed. He was always like, "No co-sleeping." Karen continued, "He was awful. He was into scare tactics. He was like, 'you're going to kill your children.' They seem to have survived! [laughs] Because co-sleeping when done safely is safe. There are scenarios of course, when it's not safe, and people shouldn't be doing it."

Samantha explained how she and Anthony picked a doctor in part based on their approach to co-sleeping. She said, "We sort of chose a pediatrician that a lot of parents at our midwife practice seemed to, just because we heard that they were a little bit more 'crunchy' attachment parenting, a little bit more friendly to that. We did like a meet-and-greet with them, before we decided we were OK with that." Although they planned a homebirth with a midwife, an extended labor precipitated a transfer to the hospital. Despite having support from their midwife and pediatrician, nurses can interfere with their plans to co-sleep. They explained:

ANTHONY: They had this little pull-out chair that sort of turned into a bed. It's like a foot off the ground, so it's not like you're up and it's dangerous. I would just lay with him on that. Lay with him on my chest, and he's not going anywhere and they come in and they're basically like, you need to put him over here.

SAMANTHA: And if you're gonna fall asleep, someone has to be awake.

ANTHONY: Yeah. It was very frustrating because we'd just get him to sleep and then they'd come in and they saw us like that. We'd be, like, "OK," and we'd get up, and then we'd go lie right back down with him. So we kind of cheated around the hospital. But that sort of fed into [it] again, like you're not supposed to do this. It's dangerous.

Becky's three-year-old daughter "sneaks in" to her bed every night. Rather than voicing disapproval, her pediatrician was encouraging. Becky said, "I brought it up with my pediatrician, and she was very supportive. She is the one who told me [to] do whatever gets everyone the most sleep. At our last check-up, she asked about our sleep and I said she spends about half the night in her own bed. And she's, like, "That's great!" And it kind of made me feel a lot better that maybe what I'm doing isn't so horrible or totally damaging." [*laughs*]

Amy, who has twin girls, also had a pediatrician supportive of co-sleeping. I asked if she had ever discussed co-sleeping. She said,

> We were comfortable bringing it up. It was in the context of their annual physical. One of the girls had some behavioral issues we were concerned about. He was very supportive and empathetic and reassured us that it was more a matter of whether we were okay with it or not. If we weren't okay with it, then we should take steps to correct it. But, if we were willing to let it go for a while that was okay, too.

Reactions from Family

Sandra's mother-in-law responded negatively when she found out she was sleeping with her one-year-old son. Sandra said, "She's very vocal about it. She lets me know. She's always the one who tells us, 'you're just spoiling him, you're ruining him. He's a baby, he needs to care about himself!'" Her own mom is supportive. Sandra said she's "OK with it" and "doesn't have anything judgmental to say." Gina described her sister's reaction to learning she and her children co-slept: "One of my sisters voiced her opinions about it. And she has never had her kids in the bed. And she said any marital problems can be solved by having your own bed. I see what she's talking about maybe once a month. And the rest of the time I think, 'Mmm, . . . we have different kinds of kids.'"

Janet is a married mother with three children, ages five, three, and one. Janet's family also voiced concerns.

> People say that all the time their moms and grandmas always said that "you're gonna spoil that baby if you don't put her down." A lot of my friends do co-sleep with their child. And

the ones who aren't parents will bring up—before I had my son, when I was pregnant, they'd say—"Well there's SIDS. . . . I think I'd be scared of rolling over on him. Did you hear about the parent that, you know, killed two of their kids?"

Sarah, the single mother mentioned above, said, "Sometimes the older generation has different feelings about kids and parents, you know, always being in separate beds and letting kids cry it out and kind of the old-fashioned ways of doing things." She continued, "I've never really let my kids cry it out for longer than twenty minutes. I don't feel like that's appropriate or right."

Stacy and her husband are originally from China. Stacy talked about her family's sleeping arrangements when she was a child, and her parents' feelings about co-sleeping. This interview once again illustrates cultural differences in attitudes about co-sleeping.

INTERVIEWER: What about when you were growing up? What were the sleeping arrangements like for your family?

STACY: On the same bed. On one bed [with] my big older sister, my mom, my dad. My mom told me we were on the same bed. My earliest memory was in the same room, but one big bed.

INTERVIEWER: Was it pretty normal back in China where you're from? Is that what people do?

STACY: Yes, I think so.

INTERVIEWER: What were your parents' thoughts on your sleeping arrangements, or your husband's parents when they came to visit? Did they have anything to say about that?

STACY: Yes. When my daughter was born I kept her in the bassinet in the same room with me but my mom always said,

"She should sleep with me, co-sleep with me." She thinks that way the baby sleeps better.

INTERVIEWER: Did your doctor, your pediatrician, have anything to say about where your child should be sleeping or did you ever talk to them about it?

STACY: Yes, yes. They kept saying let them sleep by themselves on the separate bed.

INTERVIEWER: Do you ever talk to friends of yours about their kids' sleeping arrangements? Is there any difference or do they have anything to say about things that they do?

STACY: Yes, usually moms will sit together, we'll talk about these kind of things. And lots of parents are just like us. Same way. People say they are [in] the same bed in same room.

Whether or not the parents co-sleep was shaped by whether they themselves co-slept with their own parents. The following comes from Linda, a married, Native American mother with a two-year-old daughter.

INTERVIEWER: In your social circle—family, friends, doctors . . . Do they know about the co-sleeping thing you guys are doing?

LINDA: Yes.

INTERVIEWER: Do they have any feelings about it that they shared with you?

LINDA: Um, both of our sets of parents co-slept with us.

INTERVIEWER: Really?

LINDA: So, yeah. That's kind of [a] big joke, because my mom's like, . . . "You guys always slept with us."

INTERVIEWER: And what does that mean, "You always slept with us"?

LINDA: I mean my mom would put me to bed and she would be out in the living room, and she would turn around and I would be right there. And so she was like, "You just came. It was just easier because you would sleep here and you wouldn't sleep in your crib."

INTERVIEWER: So you slept with both your parents?

LINDA: Yeah Well, no. My parents worked opposite shifts, so I would sleep with my mom and then my dad would take over when my mom had to go to work. My dad worked nights, my mom worked days. So I'm not really quite sure where I slept. I think my dad probably just let me sleep wherever I wanted.

Friends and Others

Similar to the reactions of pediatricians and parents, the friends of co-sleeping parents showed a range of reactions—some positive, some negative, and some neutral. Allison said, "I talked about it with people. The same questions are, 'Are you worried? You're going crush them. How do you sleep?'" Ingrid also talked with her friends' about co-sleeping. While supportive, they did not co-sleep themselves. She said, "a lot of my friends I think are supportive. I have a lot of friends who will say, 'My kids didn't sleep at all at night' or 'My kids never sleep at night' or whatever. With babies or newborns I always think, just bring them in your bed. I mean you can't expect her to just be happy in her own bed by herself."

Whereas Ingrid was confident in her decision to co-sleep, the negative attitudes of others may produce uncertainty for other parents. Janice is married and has a two-year-old son. She said that what "we try to create is just [my husband] and me in our bedroom and [our son] in his bedroom. The reason why we do that is because we've had family andfriends do the co-sleeping and they warned us not to start it." [*laughs*] Becky had a similar experience.

> I've had friends who say that and it kind of makes you feel bad. Like I'm a terrible parent or what's wrong with me that I can't [make] everybody happy in their own bed. I had a co-worker tell me, "Oh, I'd never let my child do that." And it just kind of shut me up right there. You know the way she was saying it, it's almost like it's kind of judgmental—like, I'm going to look down on you because that's what you are doing.

Gina said that when people express negative attitudes toward co-sleeping, she gives what she calls the "culture card" excuse:

> When he was born we only had one room. And so there wasn't much room period. We did have this little portable crib right next to the bed and I still slept with my head on the top of that thing. And I'm like, this is just ridiculous and I was just so afraid of him turning to the side, and SIDS and then I put him in bed with me and people said, "Aren't you afraid of SIDS! You shouldn't put your kid in bed!"

CONCLUSION

Societies have a stake in the manner in which children are raised. These stakeholders included doctors and nurses, family members, and friends. You could even include the media here. These groups can be powerful forces in the lives of parents. As discussed at the beginning of this chapter, co-sleeping is a controversial practice in the United States, despite its widespread acceptance around the world. My interviews with parents revealed that they were quite aware of the debate over co-sleeping and that they were engaging in a parenting practice of which many disapproved. Within this social context, it is not surprising, then, that many parents reported mixed feelings and anxiety about disclosing to others that they co-slept. Indeed, all the parents in this book reported being on the receiving end of negative comments at least once from family, friends, or medical professionals. Parents reacted in various ways. Whereas some parents stated that they simply disregarded them, other parents were embarrassed. Some parents engaged in *covert* co-sleeping, because they either assumed people would disapprove or knew in advance that they would.

That doesn't mean that parents never received positive support, because many had. Many parents were not afraid to tell (at least some) people that they co-slept, and some even promoted co-sleeping to friends. The interviews also revealed, as reported in previous studies, cultural differences in attitudes toward co-sleeping, with nonwhite and non-native parents generally receiving more support from family and friends. For example, some of these parents reported that some of their family members were confused and even expressed shock that they were *not* co-sleeping.

Despite the lack of strong evidence linking co-sleeping to negative child outcomes, one of the main concerns with co-sleeping is its safety. American parents are sometimes accused of being overly cautious about the safety of their children, yet when children fail, it is assumed the parents have made poor decisions.[5] Then there is American society's obsession with competition to consider—parents' competition over their children's developmental milestones in particular. For example, Matthew said, "I think we're definitely the minority families because we hear so many times, 'Oh, my child started sleeping through the night at eight weeks, and ten weeks, and twelve weeks,' and I'm just like, 'Okay, go away,' because we don't want to hear that."

Parents often consult with other parents, family, and friends regarding parenting issues and their children's health, but co-sleeping is sometimes left out of these important conversations.[6] Open communication between parents and their children's health care provider, especially when it comes to younger children, is also vital. Because children cannot speak for themselves, parents and doctors must collaborate as to what is best for the child, a collaboration dependent upon open communication. However, many studies indicate that patients (in this case, parents) often do not reveal their greatest concerns to physicians.[7]

At first glance, the reactions parents receive when they tell others they are co-sleeping seem relatively benign. Yet, the ability to openly discuss parenting issues with doctors, family, and friends has important consequences. It is well-known that parents who receive less social support from others report significantly higher parental stress.[8] Receiving negative messages about co-sleeping, especially from close relations and other people parents respect, may contribute to this stress. Some parents in the study reported having a very fussy child who would not sleep or cried out for their parents from their crib or bed. Although many of these parents very much wanted to co-sleep, they did so reluctantly as a result of these negative messages and fear that they were "doing the wrong thing." Poor infant sleep has been found to be a family stressor and a risk factor for maternal depression.[9] Parents who report strained relationships with and lack of support from extended family members also report more troubled sleep.[10] A Swedish study found that newlyweds were happier when parents and relatives were supportive of their parenting decisions.[11] Support from parents and extended kin is associated with marital satisfaction in early marriage.[12]

This book has covered many aspects of co-sleeping, including when and where parents and children sleep, how parents feel about co-sleeping with their children, the effect of co-sleeping on intimacy and relationships, and the extent to which parents are open with others about co-sleeping with their children. The next chapter provides a summary of the key findings about co-sleeping in families, their implications for policy and practice, and avenues for future research.

6

THE FUTURE OF CO-SLEEPING IN THE UNITED STATES

In May 2015, three infants in Des Moines, Iowa, died within a four-day period. The following week, the local newspaper's headline read, "Co-Sleeping Blamed in Death of Three D.M. Babies."[1] In the first case, the mother fell asleep while feeding her three-month-old child a bottle. In the second, a couple sleeping with their two-month-old child on an air mattress awoke to find the child unresponsive. In the third, an eight-week-old baby who had been sleeping on a mattress with his father and his father's girlfriend was found not breathing. In all cases, co-sleeping was determined by the authorities to be the culprit. To be sure, co-sleeping is associated with infant deaths and specifically sudden infant death syndrome or SIDS, and some parents are unaware of the risks. Perhaps it is just media hype, but it was clear in my interviews that the dangers of co-sleeping were a constant and ominous presence for parents. In a video that made the rounds on social media, rather than bringing his crying baby into his bed, the father climbed into his baby's crib (at which point she promptly fell asleep).

Co-Sleeping: Parents, Children, and Musical Beds is not intended to make a determination about whether co-sleeping is safe or not, or to offer medical advice. Instead, given the prevalence of co-sleeping, whether intentional or not, and the importance of sleep to our well-being, this book aims to understand what really happens in families behind closed doors. The book simply explores co-sleeping in American families—specifically co-sleeping families' nighttime patterns and routines, parents' perspectives on co-sleeping with their children, how co-sleeping affects relationships with spouses and partners, and parents' level of openness with others about the fact that they were co-sleeping. This study, really the first of its kind, provides a large amount of new and rich data on the topic.

Co-Sleeping: Parents, Children, and Musical Beds counters many myths and misconceptions that surround parents and children who sleep together. One of the most notable was that co-sleepers are not who we think they are. They are not, as one dad put it, "a bunch of hippies." Most could be described as conventional parents. Most were not following a specific parenting philosophy that promoted co-sleeping. Rather, most of the parents in the study "slid" or "drifted" into co-sleeping. With the exception of a few parents who co-slept with their children from the day they brought them home from the hospital, almost none could pinpoint the exact moment when their child started sleeping with them. They didn't have a plan to get in and didn't have a plan to get out.

The parents I interviewed provide evidence of the dynamic and diverse nature of families' nighttime activities. The sheer volume and variety of their sleeping arrangements was astounding: parents and children sleeping on the floor, children sleeping together, and parents sleeping apart just to name a few. As many parents expressed, parenting is "a 24/7 job" extending beyond daytime hours. For parents with young children, nighttime is a busy, productive time. Parents are aware of this truth, but family scientists have been slower to catch on. Hopefully, this book will stimulate more research on the "forgotten third" of a family's day (i.e., the eight hours we are assumed to be sleeping). Given the mounting evidence about the importance of sleep to individual and family well-being, this research is especially important.

All the parents in the study could name at least some benefits to co-sleeping: promoting intimacy with their children through cuddling, talking, and playing, as well as through physical contact during sleep itself; an increased sense of security of their child's safety; an expression of love for their child, spouse or partner, and family; and providing a way to spend time with their children. Conversely, all the parents in the study could name downsides to co-sleeping, including their sleep being constantly interrupted by children coming in; being squeezed or pushed out of the bed; experiencing reduced physical intimacy with their spouse or partner; disapproval from relatives, friends, and doctors; and a general sense that they are doing something they shouldn't.

Regardless of their initial intentions, the vast majority of the parents I interviewed were ambivalent about having their children in the bed. Some co-sleeping parents were even philosophically opposed to the practice. However, although co-sleeping involved many sacrifices for parents, they tended to take the long view. In my interviews, co-sleeping was generally couched in discussions of the rigors of parenting. As described in chapter 3, many parents framed their children's sleep in terms of "work." Getting their children to sleep soundly through the night can therefore be viewed as an accomplishment, reflecting the Western idea that sleep can be taught, and *learned*.

The results presented in this book are consistent with those of others' in terms of uncovering cultural differences in co-sleeping patterns and perceptions. Parents of Asian and Latin American descent were more blasé about co-sleeping than American-born parents and did not express the same level of concern about SIDS. This is not to say that non-native parents *wanted* to co-sleep, as several of them expressed the desire for their children to sleep in their own beds. It's just that their feelings about the topic were less negative (or positive) and intense.

The results of the study also supported previous research on how family structure affects co-sleeping. Although not able to determine whether co-sleeping is more prevalent among divorced or single parents, the ones in my study expressed the idea that co-sleeping provided comfort to their children and themselves. The absence of a spouse or partner created fewer barriers to having their children in the bed.

Fathers have been largely neglected from research on co-sleeping so hearing their voices on the topic was particularly important. The fathers I interviewed were active and knowledgeable participants in their families' nighttime routines, including co-sleeping. They expressed the same joys of and frustrations with co-sleeping as did mothers. Although they were perhaps less inclined to want to co-sleep than were mothers, fathers were not "brutes" about having their kids in the bed, and did not seem to me overly concerned about co-sleeping preventing them from sexual intimacy with their wives.

Clearly though, making time for sexual intimacy was important. Nearly all the parents in the study brought up this issue. However, they worked around it, figured out other times and places for sex, and generally considered having less sex a temporary situation. My interviews with parents did not resolve the question of whether co-sleeping positively or negatively affects intimacy between spouses and partners. On the one hand, many parents expressed how co-sleeping brought them closer to their partner. On the other hand, co-sleeping created distance both in terms of physical proximity and emotionally. Marital intimacy soon after the birth of a child is a complicated topic for parents, whether they co-sleep or not. As mentioned by many parents, how co-sleeping affects *family* intimacy is also an important topic to explore.

All the parents in the book described negative reactions from others about co-sleeping. They were remarkably good-natured about it. Still, many parents co-slept "covertly" or would pick and choose who to tell. Stories of mothers defending co-sleeping appear on a regular basis online and in the media. In a 2015 article that appeared in *The Huffington Post*, one co-sleeping mother said that, "telling people I sleep with my daughter is like saying I let her smoke crack."[2] In an article that appeared in *Woman's Day*, another mom said, "We've heard it all. We're spoiling them, we'll make them too attached." She maintained that co-sleeping has helped them as opposed to hurt them. Her husband agreed. He said, "I honestly don't mind. [My wife] and I still make time for sex. I don't need to sleep in the same bed as my wife every night to have intimacy with her."[3] Rather than creating additional conflict, most of the parents in my study chose to simply tolerate such attitudes.

One must keep in mind some cautions regarding the study parameters and the data that formed the basis of my findings. Despite my attempts to create a diverse sample, the families in the study are largely white, college educated, and middle-class. I did not interview low-income parents who have no choice but to co-sleep as a result of having too few bedrooms or beds. Most are mothers and the sample was drawn from Midwestern parents. The study does not provide data on the proportion of parents who co-sleep, whether their numbers are increasing or decreasing, or whether co-sleeping is good or bad for parents, children, and relationships. Incidentally, of the fifty or so children I personally met, none seemed maladjusted. Rather, they were very happy, energetic, social children.

Again, not to be underestimated is that in the United States, families who co-sleep are doing so in a context of social norms that are largely disapproving of, and at minimum are ambivalent about, this practice. The debate over co-sleeping shows no signs of abating. In a 2015 article on "clip on beds" being tried by maternity wards in the Netherlands (especially useful for women who have had C-sections and are yet not mobile), an OB-GYN from New York University commented, "If the mother rolls over from exhaustion, there would be the risk of smothering the baby. The mother's arm could go into that space in her sleep and cover the baby, or she could knock a pillow to the side and it's on the baby."[4] With such dire warnings of even the most unlikely of events, it shouldn't be surprising that feelings of anxiety, guilt, and uncertainty were common among parents.

Since 2010 the intensive parenting model and the pressure to be a "perfect parent" has experienced pushback. Books like *The Overparenting Epidemic* by George Glass and David Tabatsky and *How to Raise an Adult* by Julie Lythcott-Haims have become bestsellers.[5] However, intensive parenting, now well established, is going to be a difficult trend to reverse, leaving many American parents uncertain about what to do and how to do it. Parents should be supported and we should celebrate the diversity of modern parenting as opposed to fueling debates over the "right" way to parent. In this case, the issue is co-sleeping. So, rather than making judgments, it's time to cut parents some slack.

APPENDIX

Characteristics of the Interviewees

	Frequency	Percent
Gender[a]		
Male	13	25
Female	38	75
Age		
20–29	11	22
30–39	28	55
40 and over	9	17
Not provided	3	6
Race		
White	41	80
Black	2	4
Hispanic	3	6
Asian	3	6
Other	2	4
Number of Children		
One	17	33
Two	23	45
Three or more	11	22
Gender of Children		
All girls	10	20
All boys	22	43
Mix of girls and boys	19	37
Age of Children[b]		
2 or younger	29	29
3–5	33	33
6–8	22	22
9–12	9	9
13 and over	8	8
Residence of Children[b]		
In home	87	86
Out of home	7	7
In home part-time	7	7
Relationship to Children[b]		
Biological parent	92	91
Adopted parent	7	7
Stepparent	2	2
Relationship Status[c]		
Single, not currently dating	1	2
Single, dating	3	6
Single, serious romantic partner	2	4
Cohabiting	6	12
Married	39	76

	Frequency	Percent
Education		
High school	2	4
Some college	17	33
Four-year degree	12	24
Greater than four-year degree	20	39
Employment Status		
Part-time	13	25
Full-time	28	55
Stay-at-home parent	10	19
Flexibility in Job Hours		
None	3	6
Some	19	37
A lot	19	37
Stay-at-home parent	10	20
Work Nonstandard Hours		
Yes	34	67
No	7	14
Stay-at-home parent	10	20
Religious Affiliation		
Catholic	4	8
Protestant	7	14
Jewish	3	6
Other	12	23
None	25	49
Church Attendance		
Do not attend	23	45
Yearly	15	29
Monthly	8	16
Weekly	5	10
Income		
Less than $25,000	6	12
$25,000–$49,999	9	18
$50,000–$74,999	15	29
$75,000–$99,999	13	25
$100,000 and more	7	14
Not provided	1	2

[a] Sample includes eleven couples (N = 51).
[b] Categories are not mutually exclusive and equal the total number of children of any age of the participants (N = 101).
[c] Seven participants experienced a divorce. Among cohabiting respondents, four were cohabiting with their child(ren)'s biological father.

NOTES

1. CO-SLEEPING IN THE UNITED STATES

1. Gabriela R. Barajas et al., "Mother-Child Bed-Sharing in Toddlerhood and Cognitive and Behavioral Outcomes," *Pediatrics* 128 (2011): e339–47.

2. Task Force on Sudden Infant Death Syndrome, "SIDS and Other Sleep-Related Infant Deaths: Expansion of Recommendations for a Safe Infant Sleeping Environment," *Pediatrics* 128 (2011): e1341–67. Room sharing without bedsharing is recommended, however.

3. "Crying it out" is sometimes referred to as the "Ferber Method." However, in *Solve Your Child's Sleep Problems*, author Richard Ferber says this is an unfortunate depiction of his methods. In the 2006 edition of his book (first published in 1985), Ferber clearly states that he does not advocate or endorse "crying it out." Rather, he says, his sleep-training techniques are designed to *minimize* crying. In the new edition, he provides parents with a thorough review of the scientific literature on the health advantages and disadvantages of co-sleeping (and specific steps parents can take to reduce the risk of SIDS), so parents can make an informed decision about whether to co-sleep. Richard Ferber, *Solve Your Child's Sleep Problems*, rev. ed. (New York: Simon and Schuster, 2006).

4. Ashley Nichols Guttoso, "10 Parenting Debates to Hash Out before Baby," *Parents*, accessed January 1, 2016, http://www.parents.com/parenting/better-parenting/advice/parenting-debates/#page=7.

5. Danielle Teller and Astro Teller, "How American Parenting Is Killing the American Marriage," *Huffington Post*, September 30, 2014, http://www.huffingtonpost.com/2014/10/01/how-american-parenting-is_n_5916064.html.

6. Moreover, some parents misunderstand the recommendations, which can result in unsafe sleep habits, such as using soft bedding around an infant. See Taiwo Ajao et al., "Decisions of Black Parents about Infant Bedding and Sleep Surfaces: A Qualitative Study," *Pediatrics* 128 (2011): 494–502; Matthew Chung et al., "Safe Infant Sleep Recommendations on the Internet: Let's Google It," *Journal of Pediatrics* 161 (2012): 1080–84.

7. Eve R. Colson et al., "Trends and Factors Associated with Infant Bed Sharing, 1993–2010: The National Infant Sleep Position Study," *JAMA Pediatrics* 167 (2013): 1032–37.

8. Karen N. Pert, "Baby-Bed-Sharing Trend on the Rise, but Healthcare Providers Can Help Reverse Trend," *Yale News*, September 30, 2013, http://news.yale.edu/2013/09/30/baby-bed-sharing-rise-healthcare-providers-can-help-reverse-trend.

9. Michael J. Breus, "Co-Sleeping Increases despite Risks and Recommendations," *Psychology Today*, October 24, 2013, https://www.psychologytoday.com/blog/sleep-newzzz/201310/co-sleeping-increases-despite-risks-and-recommendations.

10. James J. McKenna, "Sudden Infant Death Syndrome in Cross-Cultural Perspective: Is Infant-Parent Co-Sleeping Protective?," *Annual Review of Anthropology* 25 (1996): 201–16.

11. Stephen M. Weimer et al., "Prevalence, Predictors, and Attitudes toward Co-Sleeping in an Urban Pediatric Center," *Clinical Pediatrics* 41 (2002): 433–38.

12. Marian F. MacDorman, Donna L. Hoyert, and T. J. Mathews, "Recent Declines in Infant Mortality in the United States, 2005–2011," *NCHS Data Brief* 120 (2013): 1–8.

13. Marian F. MacDorman et al., "International Comparisons of Infant Mortality and Related Factors: United States and Europe," *National Vital Statistics Reports* 63 (2014), accessed December 3, 2016, http://www.cdc.gov/nchs/data/nvsr/nvsr63/nvsr63_05.pdf.

14. Centers for Disease Control and Prevention, "Sudden and Unexpected Infant Death (SUID)," accessed December 3, 2016, http://www.cdc.gov/sids/pdf/sudden-unexpected-infant-death.pdf.

15. Centers for Disease Control and Prevention, "Sudden and Unexpected Infant Death and Sudden Infant Death Syndrome," February 8, 2016, accessed December 3, 2016, http://www.cdc.gov/sids/data.htm. Whereas rates of SIDS declined during this period, deaths due to unspecified causes and accidental suffocation and strangulation increased. However, researchers attribute this discrepancy to be the result of more careful investigation of these deaths as well as medical examiners' stricter adherence to SIDS definitions.

16. Ilan Behm et al., "Increasing Prevalence of Smoke-Free Homes and Decreasing Rates of Sudden Infant Death Syndrome in the United States: An Ecological Association Study," *Tobacco Control* 21 (2012): 6–11; Fern R. Hauck et al., "The Contribution of Prone Sleeping Position to the Racial Disparity in Sudden Infant Death Syndrome: The Chicago Infant Mortality Study," *Pediatrics* 110 (2002): 772–80; McKenna, "Sudden Infant Death Syndrome"; James J. McKenna, Helen L. Ball, and Lee T. Gettler, "Mother-Infant Co-Sleeping, Breastfeeding and Sudden Infant Death Syndrome: What Biological Anthropology Has Discovered about Normal Infant Sleep and Pediatric Sleep Medicine," *Yearbook of Physical Anthropology* 50 (2007): 133.

17. Felicia Trachtenberg et al., "Risk Factor Changes for Sudden Infant Death Syndrome after Initiation of Back-to-Sleep Campaign," *Pediatrics* 129 (2012): 630–38.

18. Diana Adis Tahhan, "Depth and Space in Sleep: Intimacy, Touch and the Body in Japanese Co-Sleeping Rituals," *Body & Society* 14 (2008): 37–56.

19. Task Force on Sudden Infant Death Syndrome, "SIDS and Other Sleep-Related Infant Deaths: Updated 2016 Recommendations for a Safe Infant Sleeping Environment," *Pediatrics* 138 (2016): e20162938; Tara Haelle, "New Guidelines Acknowledge the Reality: Babies Do Sleep in Mom's Bed," *National Public Radio*, October 25, 2016, http://www.npr.org/sections/health-shots/2016/10/25/499290404/new-guidelines-acknowledge-the-reality-babies-do-sleep-in-moms-bed.

20. Betsey Lozoff, George L. Askew, and Abraham W. Wolf, "Co-Sleeping and Early Childhood Sleep Problems: Effects of Ethnicity and Socioeconomic Status," *Journal of Developmental & Behavioral Pediatrics* 17 (1996): 9–15; Deborah Madansky and Craig Edelbrock, "Co-Sleeping in a Community Sample of 2- and 3-Year-Old Children," *Pediatrics* 86 (1990): 197–203; Jodi A. Mindell et al., "Parental Behaviors

and Sleep Outcomes in Infants and Toddlers: A Cross-Cultural Comparison," *Sleep Medicine* 11 (2010): 393–99.

21. Marie J. Hayes et al., "Bedsharing, Temperament, and Sleep Disturbance in Early Childhood," *Sleep* 24 (2001): 657–64.

22. Daphna Dollberg, Orly Shalev, and Pascale Chen, "'Someone's Been Sleeping in My Bed!' Parental Satisfaction Associated with Solitary and Parent-Child Co-Sleeping in Israeli Families with Young Children," *Early Child Development and Care* 180 (2010): 869–78.

23. Rosemary Messmer, Lynn D. Miller, and Christine M. Yu, "The Relationship between Parent-Infant Bed Sharing and Marital Satisfaction for Mothers of Infants," *Family Relations* 61 (2012): 798–810.

24. Sara Latz, Abraham W. Wolf, and Betsy Lozoff, "Co-Sleeping in Context: Sleep Practices and Problems in Young Children in Japan and the United States," *Archives of Pediatrics & Adolescent Medicine* 153 (1999): 339–46.

25. Xianchen Liu et al., "Sleep Patterns and Sleep Problems among Schoolchildren in the United States and China," *Pediatrics* 115, Supplement 1 (2005): 241–49.

26. Paul Okami, Thomas Weisner, and Richard Olmstead, "Outcome Correlates of Parent-Child Bedsharing: An Eighteen-Year Longitudinal Study," *Journal of Developmental & Behavioral Pediatrics* 23 (2002): 244–53.

27. Pauline W. Jansen et al., "Does Disturbed Sleeping Precede Symptoms of Anxiety or Depression in Toddlers? The Generation R Study," *Psychosomatic Medicine* 73 (2011): 242–49.

28. Helen Ball, "Parent-Infant Bed-Sharing Behavior: Effects of Feeding Type and Presence of Father," *Human Nature* 17 (2006): 301–18; Roseriet Beijers, J. Marianne Riksen-Walraven, and Carolina de Weerth, "Cortisol Regulation in 12-Month-Old Human Infants: Associations with the Infants' Early History of Breastfeeding and Co-Sleeping," *Stress* 16 (2013): 267–77; McKenna, "Sudden Infant Death Syndrome"; Wendy Middlemiss et al., "Asynchrony of Mother-Infant Hypothalamic-Pituitary-Adrenal Axis Activity following Extinction of Infant Crying Responses Induced during the Transition to Sleep," *Early Human Development* 88 (2012): 227–32; M. S. Tollenaar et al., "Solitary Sleeping in Young Infants Is Associated with Heightened Cortisol Reactivity to a Bathing Session but Not to a Vaccination," *Psychoneuroendocrinology* 37 (2012): 167–77.

29. James P. Henry and Sheila Wang, "Effects of Early Stress on Adult Affiliative Behavior," *Psychoneuroendocrinology* 23 (1998): 863–75; Daniel J. Siegel, *The Developing Mind* (New York: Guilford Press, 1999).

30. Jansen et al., "Does Disturbed Sleeping Precede Symptoms."

31. Joanne C. Crawford, "Parenting Practices in the Basque Country: Implications of Infant and Childhood Sleeping Location for Personality Development," *Ethos* 22 (1994): 42–82; John F. Forbes, David S. Weiss, and Raymond A. Folen, "The Co-Sleeping Habits of Military Children," *Military Medicine* 157 (1992): 196–200; Barry S. Hewlett and Michael E. Lamb, *Hunter-Gatherer Childhoods: Evolutionary, Developmental, and Cultural Perspectives* (Piscataway, NJ: Transaction Publishers, 2005).

32. Middlemiss et al., "Asynchrony of Mother-Infant."

33. Carol Potter and John Carpenter, "Fathers' Involvement in Sure Start: What Do Fathers and Mothers Perceive as the Benefits?," *Practice: Social Work in Action* 22 (2010): 3–15; William Sears, *Becoming a Father: How to Nurture and Enjoy Your Family*, rev. ed. (Franklin Park, IL: La Leche League International, 2003).

34. Sears, *Becoming a Father*.

35. Morgen Peck, "How Co-Sleeping with an Infant Might Make You a Better Dad," *Scientific American Mind* 23 (2013): 8.

36. Eyal Abraham et al., "Father's Brain Is Sensitive to Childcare Experiences," *Proceedings of the National Academy of Sciences* 111 (2014): 9792–97.

37. Jodi A. Mindell et al., "Parental Behaviors and Sleep Outcomes."

38. Jodi A. Mindell et al., "A Nightly Bedtime Routine: Impact on Sleep in Young Children and Maternal Mood," *Sleep* 32 (2009): 599.

39. Jackson, Deborah. *Three in a Bed: The Benefits of Sharing Your Bed with Your Baby* (New York: Bloomsbury, 1999); James J. McKenna, *Sleeping with Your Baby* (Washington, DC: Platypus Media, 2007).

40. Mayim Bialik, *Beyond the Sling* (New York: Simon and Schuster, 2012).

41. Bruce Feiler, "Married but Sleeping Alone," *The New York Times*, July 25, 2010, http://www.nytimes.com/2010/07/25/fashion/25FamilyMatters.html.

42. Moreover, co-sleeping is probably underreported due to the stigma that surrounds the practice.

43. National Sleep Foundation, *2014 Sleep in America Poll*, National Sleep Foundation, March 2014, accessed January 1, 2016, http://sleepfoundation.org/sites/default/files/2014-NSF-Sleep-in-America-poll-summary-of-findings---FINAL-Updated-3-26-14-.pdf.

44. Kathleen Dyer Ramos, Davin Youngclarke, and Jane E. Anderson, "Parental Perceptions of Sleep Problems among Co-Sleeping and Solitary Sleeping Children," *Infant and Child Development* 16 (2007): 417–31.

45. Carrie K.Shapiro-Mendoza et al., "Trends in Infant Bedding Use: National Infant Sleep Position Study, 1993–2010," *Pediatrics* (2014): peds-2014.

46. The same poll reported that 16 percent of infants, 11 percent of toddlers, 16 percent of preschoolers, and 5 percent of school-aged children woke up in their parents' bed in the morning. Overall, 43 percent of infants, 27 percent of toddlers, 28 percent of preschoolers, and 14 percent of school-aged children changed location during the night.

47. Oskar G. Jenni et al., "A Longitudinal Study of Bed Sharing and Sleep Problems among Swiss Children in the First 10 Years of Life," *Pediatrics* 115 (2005): 233–40.

48. Attachment Parenting International, "Infant Sleep Safety," accessed January 1, 2015, http://www.attachmentparenting.org/infantsleepsafety.

49. Forbes, Weiss, and Folen, "The Co-Sleeping Habits"; Madansky and Edelbrock, "Co-Sleeping in a Community Sample."

50. Tine Thevenin. *The Family Bed* (New York: Perigee Trade, 2003).

51. See, for example, Dollberg, Shalev, and Chen, "'Someone's Been Sleeping in My Bed!'"; Oskar G. Jenni and Bonnie B. O'Connor, "Children's Sleep: An Interplay between Culture and Biology," *Pediatrics* 115 (2005): 204–16; Tahhan, "Depth and Space in Sleep."

52. For example see Andrew J. Cherlin, *The Marriage-Go-Round* (New York: Vintage Books, 2009); Jennifer Glass and Philip Levchak, "Red States, Blue States, and Divorce: Understanding the Impact of Conservative Protestantism on Regional Variation in Divorce Rates," *American Journal of Sociology* 119 (2014): 1002–46; Amy T. Schalet, *Not Under My Roof: Parents, Teens, and the Culture of Sex* (Chicago: University of Chicago Press, 2011); Eric Luis Uhlmann and Jeffrey

Sanchez-Burks, "The Implicit Legacy of American Protestantism," *Journal of Cross-Cultural Psychology* 45 (2014): 992–1006.

53. Sally A. Baddock et al., "Sleep Arrangements and Behavior of Bed-Sharing Families in the Home Setting." *Pediatrics* 119 (2007): e200–e207; Ball, "Parent-Infant Bed-Sharing Behavior."

54. Jacob E. Cheadle, Paul R. Amato, and Valarie King, "Patterns of Nonresident Father Contact," *Demography* 47 (2010): 205–25; Cherine Habib et al., "The Importance of Family Management, Closeness with Father and Family Structure in Early Adolescent Alcohol Use," *Addiction* 105 (2010): 1750–58; Valarie King, Katherine C. Stamps, and Daniel N. Hawkins, "Adolescents with Two Nonresident Biological Parents: Living Arrangements, Parental Involvement, and Well-Being," *Journal of Family Issues* 31 (2009): 3–30; Natasha J. Cabrera and Catherine S. Tamis-LeMonda, *Handbook of Father Involvement: Multidisciplinary Perspectives* (London: Routledge, 2013); Jelani Mandara, Sheba Y. Rogers, and Richard E. Zinbarg, "The Effects of Family Structure on African American Adolescents' Marijuana Use," *Journal of Marriage and Family* 73 (2011): 557–69; Katherine R. Wilson and Margot R. Prior, "Father Involvement and Child Well-Being," *Journal of Pediatrics and Child Health* 47 (2011): 405–7.

55. Stephanie Milan, Stephanie Snow, and Sophia Belay, "The Context of Preschool Children's Sleep: Racial/Ethnic Differences in Sleep Locations, Routines, and Concerns," *Journal of Family Psychology* 21 (2007): 20; Lozoff, Askew, and Wolf, "Co-Sleeping and Early Childhood."

56. Madansky and Edelbrock, "Co-Sleeping in a Community Sample"; Frances Fuchs Schachter et al., "Co-Sleeping and Sleep Problems in Hispanic-American Urban Young Children," *Pediatrics* 84 (1989): 522–30.

57. Sheldon Cohen and Denise Janicki-Deverts, "Who's Stressed? Distributions of Psychological Stress in the United States in Probability Samples from 1983, 2006, and 2009," *Journal of Applied Social Psychology* 42 (2012): 1320–34; Susan Nolen-Hoeksema, "Gender Differences in Depression," *Current Directions in Psychological Science* 10 (2001): 173–76; Debra Umberson, Tetyana Pudrovska, and Corinne Reczek, "Parenthood, Childlessness, and Well-Being: A Life Course Perspective," *Journal of Marriage and Family* 72 (2010): 612–29.

58. Bureau of Labor Statistics, "Employment Characteristics of Families Summary," Bureau of Labor Statistics, April 22, 2016, accessed October 6, 2016, http://www.bls.gov/news.release/famee.nr0.htm.

59. Allison J. Pugh, *Longing and Belonging: Parents, Children, and Consumer Culture* (Oakland: University of California Press, 2009).

60. Sharon Hayes. *The Cultural Contradictions of Motherhood* (New Haven, CT: Yale University Press, 1996).

61. Margaret Nelson, "Reflections on the 25th Anniversary of the Second Shift," paper presented at the annual meeting for the American Sociological Association, San Francisco, CA, August 16–19, 2014.

62. Jenni and O'Connor, "Children's Sleep."

63. Centers for Disease Control and Prevention, "Insufficient Sleep Is a Public Health Epidemic," Centers for Disease Control, September 3, 2015, accessed January 1, 2016, http://www.cdc.gov/features/dssleep.

64. Caryl L. Gay, Kathryn A. Lee, and Shih-Yu Lee, "Sleep Patterns and Fatigue in New Mothers and Fathers," *Biological Research for Nursing* 5 (2004): 311–18.

65. National Sleep Foundation, *2013 International Bedroom Poll*, January 1, 2016, http://sleepfoundation.org/sites/default/files/RPT495a.pdf.

66. National Sleep Foundation, *2004 Children and Sleep Poll*, National Sleep Foundation, March 1, 2004, accessed January 1, 2016, http://sleepfoundation.org/sleep-polls-data/sleep-in-america-poll/2004-children-and-sleep.

67. Lisa J. Meltzer et al., "Prevalence of Diagnosed Sleep Disorders in Pediatric Primary Care Practices," *Pediatrics* 125 (2010): e1410–18.

68. Francesco P. Cappuccio et al., "Sleep Duration and All-Cause Mortality: A Systematic Review and Meta-Analysis of Prospective Studies," *Sleep* 33 (2010): 585; Julia F. Dewald et al., "The Influence of Sleep Quality, Sleep Duration and Sleepiness on School Performance in Children and Adolescents: A Meta-Analytic Review," *Sleep Medicine Reviews* 14 (2010): 179–89; Jeanine Kamphuis et al., "Poor Sleep as a Potential Causal Factor in Aggression and Violence," *Sleep Medicine* 13 (2012): 327–34; Holly J. Ramsawh et al., "Relationship of Anxiety Disorders, Sleep Quality, and Functional Impairment in a Community Sample," *Journal of Psychiatric Research* 43 (2009): 926–33; Mark R. Rosekind et al., "The Cost of Poor Sleep: Workplace Productivity Loss

and Associated Costs," *Journal of Occupational and Environmental Medicine* 52 (2010): 91–98; Karine Spiegel et al., "Effects of Poor and Short Sleep on Glucose Metabolism and Obesity Risk," *Nature Reviews Endocrinology* 5 (2009): 253–61; Wendy M. Troxel, "It's More than Sex: Exploring the Dyadic Nature of Sleep and Implications for Health," *Psychosomatic Medicine* 72 (2010): 578–86.

69. David K. Randall, *Dreamland: Adventures in the Strange Science of Sleep* (New York: W. W. Norton & Company, 2012); Kat Duff, *The Secret Life of Sleep* (New York: Atria Books, 2014).

70. Robert Meadows, "The 'Negotiated Night': An Embodied Conceptual Framework for the Sociological Study of Sleep," *Sociological Review* 53 (2005): 240–54.

71. National Sleep Foundation, *2012 Bedroom Poll*, National Sleep Foundation, April 1, 2012, accessed January 1, 2016, http://sleepfoundation.org/sites/default/files/bedroompoll/NSF_Bedroom_Poll_Report.pdf.

72. Jennifer A. Ailshire and Sarah A. Burgard, "Family Relationships and Troubled Sleep among U.S. Adults: Examining the Influences of Contact Frequency and Relationship Quality," *Journal of Health and Social Behavior* 5 (2012): 248–62; Anne Marie Meijer and Godfried L. H. van den Wittenboer, "Contribution of Infants' Sleep and Crying to Marital Relationship of First-Time Parent Couples in the 1st Year after Childbirth," *Journal of Family Psychology* 21 (2007): 49–57; Lisa J. Meltzer and Jodi A. Mindell, "Relationship between Child Sleep Disturbances and Maternal Sleep, Mood, and Parenting Stress: A Pilot Study," *Journal of Family Psychology* 21 (2007): 67; Carol M. Worthman and Ryan A. Brown, "Companionable Sleep: Social Regulation of Sleep and Co-Sleeping in Egyptian Families," *Journal of Family Psychology* 21 (2007): 124–35.

73. Paul C. Rosenblatt. *Two in a Bed: The Social System of Couple Bed Sharing* (Albany: State University of New York Press, 2006).

74. Ronald E. Dahl, and Mona El-Sheikh, "Considering Sleep in a Family Context: Introduction to the Special Issue," *Journal of Family Psychology* 21 (2007): 1–3.

75. Duff, *The Secret Life*.

76. National Sleep Foundation, *2013 International Bedroom Poll*.

77. Wanaporn Anuntaseree et al., "Night Waking in Thai Infants at 3 Months of Age: Association between Parental Practices and Infant Sleep," *Sleep Medicine* 9 (2008): 564–71.

78. Mindell et al., "Parental Behaviors"; Barbara Welles-Nystrom, "Co-sleeping as a Window into Swedish Culture: Considerations of Gender and Health Care," *Scandinavian Journal of Caring Sciences* 19 (2005): 354–60.

79. Duff, *The Secret Life*; Carol M. Worthman and Melissa K. Melby, "Toward a Comparative Developmental Ecology of Human Sleep," in *Adolescent Sleep Patterns: Biological, Social, and Psychological Influences*, ed. Mary A. Carskadon (New York: Cambridge University Press, 2002), 69–117.

80. Randall, *Dreamland*.

81. National Sleep Foundation, *2014 Sleep in America Poll*.

82. Abraham W. Wolf and Betsy Lozoff, "Object Attachment, Thumbsucking, and the Passage to Sleep," *Journal of the American Academy of Child & Adolescent Psychiatry* 28 (1989): 287–92; D. W. Winnicott, "Transitional Objects and Transitional Phenomena," *International Journal of Psycho-Analysis* 34 (1953): 89–97.

83. Duff, *The Secret Life*.

84. Xiao-na Huang et al., "Co-Sleeping and Children's Sleep in China," *Biological Rhythm Research* 41 (2010): 169–81; Gilda A. Morelli et al., "Cultural Variation in Infants' Sleeping Arrangements: Questions of Independence," *Developmental Psychology* 28 (1992): 604.

85. Jenni and O'Connor, "Children's Sleep."

86. Sadaf Farooqi, I. J. Perry, and D. G. Beevers, "Ethnic Differences in Sleeping Position and in Risk of Cot Death," *The Lancet* 338 (1991): 1455; Lozoff, Askew, and Wolf, "Co-Sleeping and Early Childhood"; Schachter, "Co-Sleeping and Sleep Problems."

87. National Sleep Foundation. *2010 Sleep in America Poll*, accessed January 1, 2016, http://sleepfoundation.org/sites/default/files/nsaw/ NSF%20Sleep%20in%20%20America%20Poll%20-%20Summary%20of%20Findings%20.pdf.

88. Crawford, "Parenting Practices in the Basque Country"; Karen Spruyt, Ivonne Anguh, and Odochi U. Nwabara, "Sleep Behavior of Underrepresented Youth," *Journal of Public Health* 22 (2014): 111–20.

89. Duff, *The Secret Life*.

90. Roger A. Ekirch, *At Day's Close: Night in Times Past* (W. W. Norton & Company, 2006), 278.

91. Ekirch, *At Day's Close*, 278.

92. Craig Koslofsky. *Evening's Empire: A History of Night in Early Modern Europe* (Cambridge: Cambridge University Press, 2011), 1.

93. Ekirch, *At Day's Close*.

94. Randall, *Dreamland*.

95. Ekirch, *At Day's Close*; Koslofsky, *Evening's Empire*. One of the mothers in my study used nighttime in that manner, often staying up until 2 a.m., "Because that's when I sew."

96. Harriet B. Presser, *Working in a 24/7 Economy: Challenges for American Families* (New York: Russell Sage Foundation, 2005).

97. Presser, *Working in a 24/7 Economy*.

98. David J. Maume, Rachel A. Sebastian, and Anthony R. Bardo, "Gender Differences in Sleep Disruption among Retail Food Workers," *American Sociological Review* 74 (2009): 989–1007; David J. Maume, Rachel A. Sebastian, and Anthony R. Bardo, "Gender, Work-Family Responsibilities, and Sleep," *Gender & Society* 24 (2010): 746–68.

99. Ariel Kalil et al., "Work Hours, Schedules, and Insufficient Sleep among Mothers and Their Young Children," *Journal of Marriage and Family* 76 (2014): 891–904; Randall, *Dreamland*; Rosenblatt, *Two in a Bed*; Colleen N. Nugent and Lindsey I. Black, "Sleep Duration, Quality of Sleep, and Use of Sleep Medication, by Sex and Family Type, 2013–2014," *NCHS Data Brief* 230 (2016): 1–8.

100. Andrew J. Weigert, *Sociology of Everyday Life* (New York: Longman, 1981).

101. Kerry Daly, "Family Theory versus Theory Families Live By," *Journal of Marriage and Family* 65 (2003): 771.

102. Daly, "Family Theory," 779.

103. Pauline Boss, "Family Stress," in *Handbook of Marriage and Family*, eds. Marvin B. Sussman and Suzanne K. Steinmets (New York: Plenum, 1987), 695–723.

104. Yoshi Iwasaki and Ingrid E. Schneider, "Leisure, Stress, and Coping: An Evolving Area of Inquiry." *Leisure Sciences* 25 (2003): 107–13; Mihaela Robila and Ambika Krishnakumar, "Economic Pressure and Children's Psychological Functioning," *Journal of Child and Family Studies* 15 (2006): 433–41; and Les B. Whitbeck, Ronald L. Simons, Rand D. Conger, K. A. S. Wickrama, Kevin A. Ackley, and

Glen H. Elder Jr., "The Effects of Parents' Working Conditions and Family Economic Hardship on Parenting Behaviors and Children's Self-Efficacy," *Social Psychology Quarterly* (1997): 291–303.

105. Urie Bronfenbrenner, *The Ecology of Human Development: Experiments by Nature and Design* (Cambridge, MA: Harvard University Press, 2009).

106. For exceptions, see Hayes et al., "Bedsharing, Temperament, and Sleep Disturbance," who include children who "sometimes" co-sleep, and Jenni et al., "A Longitudinal Study of Bed Sharing," who include children who co-sleep "at least once a week."

107. Messmer et al., "The Relationship"; Ramos et al., "Parental Perceptions."

108. Barney G. Glaser and Anselm L. Strauss, *The Discovery of Grounded Theory: Strategies for Qualitative Research* (Piscataway, NJ: Transaction Publishers, 2009); Anselm Strauss and Juliet M. Corbin, *Basics of Qualitative Research*, vol. 15 (Newbury Park, CA: Sage, 1990).

109. Johnny Saldana, *The Coding Manual for Qualitative Researchers*, 2nd ed. (Los Angeles: Sage Publications, 2013).

110. Matthew B. Miles and Michael A. Huberman, *Qualitative Data Analysis*, 2nd ed. (Thousand Oaks, CA: Sage, 1994).

111. Katherine R. Allen, "A Conscious and Inclusive Family Studies," *Journal of Marriage and Family* 62 (2000): 4.

2. CO-SLEEPING LOGISTICS

1. Baddock, "Sleep Arrangements and Behavior."

2. Ball, "Parent-Infant Bed-Sharing Behavior."

3. Rosenblatt, *Two in a Bed*.

4. Sears, *Becoming a Father*.

5. National Sleep Foundation, *2004 Sleep in America Poll*, National Sleep Foundation, March 1, 2004. Accessed February 19, 2015, https://sleepfoundation.org/sites/default/files/FINAL SOF 2004.pdf.

6. Wendy Hollway, "The Maternal Bed: Mothering and Ambivalence," in *Mothering and Ambivalence*, ed. Wendy Hollway and Brid Featherstone (New York: Routledge, 1997), 54–79.

7. Scott M. Stanley, Galena Kline Rhoades, and Howard J. Markman, "Sliding versus Deciding: Inertia and the Premarital Cohabitation Effect," *Family Relations* 55 (2006): 499–509.

8. Maume et al., "Gender Differences in Sleep Disruption"; Maume et al., "Gender, Work-Family Responsibilities."

9. Maume et al., "Gender Differences in Sleep Disruption"; Maume et al., "Gender, Work-Family Responsibilities."

3. PARENTS' PERSPECTIVES ON CO-SLEEPING

1. Chadwick Menning, "'I've Kept It That Way on Purpose': Adolescents' Management of Negative Parental Relationship Traits after Divorce and Separation," *Journal of Contemporary Ethnography* 37 (2008): 586–618. These are sometimes referred to as "dripolator" and "percolator" effects.

2. Alice S. Rossi, "Transition to Parenthood," *Journal of Marriage and the Family* (1968): 26–39.

3. India J. Ornelas et al., "Challenges and Strategies to Maintaining Emotional Health: Qualitative Perspectives of Mexican Immigrant Mothers," *Journal of Family Issues* 30 (2009): 1564.

4. Cohen and Janicki-Deverts, "Who's Stressed?"; Ingegard Hildingsson and Jan Thomas, "Parental Stress in Mothers and Fathers One Year after Birth," *Journal of Reproductive and Infant Psychology* 32 (2014): 41–56; Nolen-Hoeksema, "Gender Differences in Depression"; Umberson, Pudrovska, and Reczek, "Parenthood, Childlessness, and Well-Being."

5. Richard R. Abidin, "Introduction to the Special Issue: The Stresses of Parenting," *Journal of Clinical Child Psychology* 19 (1990): 298–301.

6. Keith A. Crnic and Christine Low, "Everyday Stresses and Parenting," in *Handbook of Parenting*, vol. 5, *Practical Issues in Parenting*, ed. Marc H. Bornstein (Mahwah, NJ: Lawrence Erlbaum and Associates, 2002), 243–67; Keith A. Crnic, Catherine Gaze, and Casey Hoffman, "Cumulative Parenting Stress across the Preschool Period: Relations to Maternal Parenting and Child Behavior at Age 5," *Infant and Child Development* 14 (2005): 117–32.

7. Kira S. Birditt, Karen L. Fingerman, and David M. Almeida, "Age Differences in Exposure and Reactions to Interpersonal Tensions: A Daily Diary Study," *Psychology and Aging* 20 (2005): 330; Paul R. Amato, "Research on Divorce: Continuing Trends and New Developments," *Journal of Marriage and Family* 72 (2010): 650–66; Susan L. Brown, "The Effect of Union Type on Psychological Well-Being: Depression among Cohabitors versus Marrieds," *Journal of Health and Social Behavior* 41 (2000): 241–55; Regina M. Bures, Tanya Koropeckyj-Cox, and Michael Loree, "Childlessness, Parenthood, and Depressive Symptoms among Middle-Aged and Older Adults," *Journal of Family Issues* 30 (2009): 670–87.

8. Margareta Widarsson et al., "Parental Stress in Early Parenthood among Mothers and Fathers in Sweden," *Scandinavian Journal of Caring Sciences* 27 (2013): 839–47.

9. Sears, *Becoming a Father.*

10. Jodi A. Mindell et al., "A Nightly Bedtime Routine," 599.

11. Rozsika Parker, *Torn in Two: The Experience of Maternal Ambivalence* (London: Virago Press, 2005).

12. Parker, *Torn in Two.*

13. Andrew Solomon, "The Secret Sadness of Pregnancy with Depression," *New York Times*, May 31, 2015, http://www.nytimes.com/2015/05/31/magazine/the-secret-sadness-of-pregnancy-with-depression.html.

14. Stephen Frosh, "Fathers' Ambivalence (Too)," *Mothering and Ambivalence*, eds. Wendy Hollway and Brid Featherstone (New York: Routledge, 1997), 37–53.

15. Parker, *Torn in Two.*

16. Rachel Margolis and Mikko Myrskylä, "Parental Well-Being Surrounding First Birth as a Determinant of Further Parity Progression," *Demography* 52 (2015): 1147–66.

17. Jane L. Rankin, *Parenting Experts: Their Advice, the Research, and Gettting It Right* (Westport, CT: Praeger Publishers, 2005), 9.

18. Alexander Thomas, Stella Chess, and Herbert George Birch, *Temperament and Behavior Disorders in Children* (New York: New York University Press, 1968); Niina Komsi et al., "Continuity of Temperament from Infancy to Middle Childhood," *Infant Behavior and Development* 29 (2006): 494–508.

19. For information on maternal stress see Pam Belluck, "'Thinking of Ways to Harm Her': New Findings on Timing and Range of Maternal Mental Illness," *New York Times*, June 15, 2014, http://www.nytimes.com/2014/06/16/health/thinking-of-ways-to-harm-her.html; Stephanie H. Parade et al., "Close Relationships Predict Curvilinear Trajectories of Maternal Depressive Symptoms over the Transition to Parenthood," *Family Relations* 63 (2014): 206–18.

20. Letitia E. Kotila, Sarah J. Schoppe-Sullivan, and Claire M. Kamp Dush, "Time Parenting Activities in Dual-Earner Families at the Transition to Parenthood," *Family Relations* 62 (2013): 795–807.

21. Jay Fagan et al., "Should Researchers Conceptualize Differently the Dimensions of Parenting for Fathers and Mothers?," *Journal of Family Theory & Review* 6 (2014): 390–405.

22. Alfred DeMaris, Annette Mahoney, and Kenneth I. Pargament, "Doing the Scut Work of Infant Care: Does Religiousness Encourage Father Involvement?," *Journal of Marriage and Family* 73 (2011): 354–68.

23. Patricia L. East, Nina C. Chien, and Jennifer S. Barber, "Adolescents' Pregnancy Intentions, Wantedness, and Regret: Cross-Lagged Relations with Mental Health and Harsh Parenting," *Journal of Marriage and Family* 74 (2012): 167–85; Tea Trillingsgaard, Katherine J. W. Baucom, and Richard E. Heyman, "Predictors of Change in Relationship Satisfaction during the Transition to Parenthood," *Family Relations* 63 (2014): 667–79.

24. Brian P. Don and Kristin D. Mickelson, "Relationship Satisfaction Trajectories across the Transition to Parenthood among Low-Risk Parents," *Journal of Marriage and Family* 76 (2014): 677–92; Erin Kramer Holmes, Takayuki Sasaki, and Nancy L. Hazen, "Smooth versus Rocky Transitions to Parenthood: Family Systems in Developmental Context," *Family Relations* 62 (2013): 824–37.

25. Roberta L. Coles, "Just Doing What They Gotta Do: Single Black Custodial Fathers Coping with the Stresses and Reaping the Rewards of Parenting, " *Journal of Family Issues* 30 (2009): 1311–38.

4. CO-SLEEPING, RELATIONSHIPS, AND INTIMACY

1. Claire M. Kamp Dush, Miles G. Taylor, and Rhiannon A. Kroeger, "Marital Happiness and Psychological Well-Being across the Life Course," *Family Relations* 57 (2008): 211–26.

2. Thomas N. Bradbury, Frank D. Fincham, and Steven R. H. Beach, "Research on the Nature and Determinants of Marital Satisfaction: A Decade in Review," *Journal of Marriage and Family* 62 (2000): 969.

3. Brian D. Doss et al., "The Effect of the Transition to Parenthood on Relationship Quality: An 8-Year Prospective Study," *Journal of Personality and Social Psychology* 6 (2009): 601.

4. Carolyn Cowan and Philip C. Cowan, "News You Can Use: Are Babies Bad for Marriage?" *Council on Contemporary Families*, January 9, 2009, https://contemporaryfamilies.org/news-can-use-babies-bad-marriage.

5. Bonnie Fox, *When Couples Become Parents* (Toronto: University of Toronto Press, 2009); Jill E. Yavorsky, Claire M. Kamp Dush, and Sarah J. Schoppe-Sullivan, "The Production of Inequality: The Gender Division of Labor across the Transition to Parenthood," *Journal of Marriage and Family* 77 (2015): 662–79.

6. Joseph G. Grzywacz et al., "Nonstandard Work Schedules and Developmentally Generative Parenting Practices: An Application of Propensity Score Techniques," *Family Relations* 60 (2011): 45–59; Wen-Jui Han and Liana E. Fox, "Parental Work Schedules and Children's Cognitive Trajectories," *Journal of Marriage and Family* 73 (2011): 962–80.

7. Sarah J. Schoppe-Sullivan et al., "Goodness-of-Fit in Family Context: Infant Temperament, Marital Quality, and Early Coparenting Behavior," *Infant Behavior and Development* 30 (2007): 82–96.

8. Messmer et al., "The Relationship between Parent-Infant Bed Sharing."

9. Anna Marie Medina, Crystal L. Lederhos, and Teresa A. Lillis, "Sleep Disruption and Decline in Marital Satisfaction across the Transition to Parenthood," *Families, Systems, & Health* 27 (2009): 153; Meijer and van den Wittenboer, "Contribution of Infants' Sleep."

10. Ailshire and Burgard, "Family Relationships and Troubled Sleep."

11. Rosenblatt, *Two in a Bed*.

12. D. H. Olson and D. M. Gorall, "Circumplex Model of Marital and Family Systems," in *Normal Family Processes*, ed. F. Walsh (New York: Guilford, 2003), 516.

13. Doss et al., "The Effect of the Transition to Parenthood," 601.

14. Doss et al., "The Effect of the Transition to Parenthood."

15. John Mordechai Gottman and Robert Wayne Levenson, "The Timing of Divorce: Predicting When a Couple Will Divorce over a 14-Year Period," *Journal of Marriage and Family* 62 (2000): 737–45.

16. Schoppe-Sullivan et al., "Goodness-of-Fit in Family Context"; Jay Teachman, "Military Service, Race, and the Transition to Marriage and Cohabitation," *Journal of Family Issues* 30 (2009): 1433–54.

17. John M. Gottman and Clifford I. Notarius, "Decade Review: Observing Marital Interaction," *Journal of Marriage and Family* 62 (2000): 927–47.

18. Emily A. Impett, Amy Muise, and Diana Peragine, "Sexuality in the Context of Relationships," *APA Handbook of Sexuality and Psychology* 1 (2013): 269–316; Tone Ahlborg and Margaretha Strandmark, "The Baby Was the Focus of Attention—First-Time Parents' Experiences of Their Intimate Relationship," *Scandinavian Journal of Caring Sciences* 15 (2001): 318–25.

19. Carolyn Cowan, and Philip A. Cowan, *When Partners Become Parents: The Big Life Change for Couples* (Mahwah, NJ: Lawrence Erlbaum Associates Publishers, 2000).

20. Malin Hansson and Tone Ahlborg, "Quality of the Intimate and Sexual Relationship in First-Time Parents—A Longitudinal Study," *Sexual & Reproductive HealthCare* 3 (2012): 21–29.

21. Megan K. Maas et al., "Division of Labor and Multiple Domains of Sexual Satisfaction among First-Time Parents," *Journal of Family Issues* (2015): doi:10.1177/0192513X15604343.

22. Rosenblatt, *Two in a Bed*, 60.

23. Martin T. Stein et al., "Co-Sleeping (Bedsharing) among Infants and Toddlers," *Journal of Developmental & Behavioral Pediatrics* 18 (1997): 408–12; Calvin Colarusso quoted on p. 409; Nancy Powers quoted on p. 411.

24. Tone Ahlborg and Margaretha Strandmark, "Factors Influencing
the Quality of Intimate Relationships Six Months after Delivery—First-
time Parents' own Views and Coping Strategies," *Journal of Psychosomatic Obstetrics & Gynecology* 27 (2006): 163–72.

25. Susan Pacey, "Couples and the First Baby: Responding to New
Parents' Sexual and Relationship Problems," *Sexual and Relationship
Therapy* 19 (2004): 223–46.

26. Sears, *Becoming a Father*, 113.

27. M. Dixon, N. Booth, and R. Powell, "Sex and Relationships following Childbirth: A First Report from General Practice of 131 Couples," *British Journal of General Practice* 50 (2000): 223–24.

28. Pacey, "Couples and the First Baby."

29. Rosenblatt, *Two in a Bed*, 58.

30. Duff, *The Secret Life of Sleep*.

31. Vanessa Reid and Mikki Meadows-Oliver, "Postpartum Depression in Adolescent Mothers: An Integrative Review of the Literature,"
Journal of Pediatric Health Care 21 (2007): 289–98.

5. OPENNESS, SECRECY, AND REACTIONS FROM OTHERS

1. Sarah Kallies, "Excuse Me While I Explain What I Meant about
Toxic Death Cream," June 22, 2016, http://sarahkallies.com/the-
inkwell/2016/6/6/excuse-me-while-i-meant-about-toxic-
death-cream.

2. Monica Östberg and Berit Hagekull, "A Structural Modeling Approach to the Understanding of Parenting Stress," *Journal of Clinical
Child Psychology* 29 (2000): 615–25.

3. Bradford W. Wilcox and Jeffrey Dew, "Motherhood and Marriage: A Response," *Journal of Marriage and Family* 73 (2011): 29–32.

4. Maureen Perry-Jenkins et al., "Working-Class Jobs and New Parents' Mental Health," *Journal of Marriage and Family* 73 (2011):
1117–32.

5. Abidin, "Introduction to the Special Issue: The Stresses of Parenting."

6. G. B. Hickson, and E. W. Clayton, "Parents and Their Doctors,"
in *Handbook of Parenting*, vol. 5, *Practical Issues in Parenting*, ed.

Marc H. Bornstein (Mahwah, NJ: Lawrence Erlbaum and Associates, 2002), 439–62.

7. Hickson and Clayton, "Parents and Their Doctors."

8. Östberg and Hagekull, "A Structural Modeling Approach."

9. Avi Sadeh, Liat Tikotzky, and Anat Scher, "Parenting and Infant Sleep," *Sleep Medicine Reviews* 14 (2010): 89–96.

10. Ailshire and Burgard, "Family Relationships and Troubled Sleep."

11. Eric D. Widmer et al., "From Support to Control: A Configurational Perspective on Conjugal Quality," *Journal of Marriage and Family* 71 (2009): 437–48.

12. Lawrence A. Kurdek, "Gender and Marital Satisfaction Early in Marriage: A Growth Curve Approach," *Journal of Marriage and Family* 67 (2005): 68–84.

6. THE FUTURE OF CO-SLEEPING IN THE UNITED STATES

1. Elmer MacKenzie, "Co-Sleep Blamed in Death of 3 D.M. Babies." *Des Moines Register*, May 22, 2015, http://www. desmoinesregister.com/story/news/crime-and-courts/2015/05/20/ babies-die-accidental-smothering-safe-sleep/27651449.

2. Laura Lifshitz, "Yes, My Daughter Sleeps with Me Sometimes, and No, I Don't Care What You Think," *Huffington Post*, April 20, 2015, http://www.huffingtonpost.com/laura-lifshitz/yes-my-daughter-sleeps-with-me-sometimes-and-no-i-dont-care-what-you-think_b_7089056.html.

3. Marlisse Cepeda, "Mom Sleeps in Same Bed as Her 9- and 10-Year-Old Sons, Says It's Better for Them." *Woman's Day*, May 19, 2015, http://www.womansday.com/relationships/family-friends/news/a50646/mom-sleeps-in-the-same-bed-as-her-nine-and-10-year-old-sons.

4. Lauren Smith, "This Maternity Bed Totally Changes a New Mom's Hospital Stay," *Good Housekeeping*, December 28, 2015, http://www.goodhousekeeping.com/life/parenting/news/a36148/new-maternity-bed-with-bassinets.

5. George S. Glass and David Tabatsky, *The Overparenting Epidemic* (New York: Skyhorse Publishing, 2014); Julie Lythcott-Haimes, *How to Raise an Adult* (New York: Macmillan, 2015).

BIBLIOGRAPHY

Abidin, Richard R. "Introduction to the Special Issue: The Stresses of Parenting." *Journal of Clinical Child Psychology* 19 (1990): 298–301.

Abraham, Eyal, Talma Hendler, Irit Shapira-Lichter, Yaniv Kanat-Maymon, Orna Zagoory-Sharon, and Ruth Feldman. "Father's Brain Is Sensitive to Childcare Experiences." *Proceedings of the National Academy of Sciences* 111 (2014): 9792–97.

Ahlborg, Tone, and Margaretha Strandmark. "The Baby Was the Focus of Attention—First-Time Parents' Experiences of Their Intimate Relationship." *Scandinavian Journal of Caring Sciences* 15 (2001): 318–25.

Ahlborg, Tone, and Margaretha Strandmark. "Factors Influencing the Quality of Intimate Relationships Six Months after Delivery—First-Time Parents' Own Views and Coping Strategies." *Journal of Psychosomatic Obstetrics & Gynecology* 27 (2006): 163–72.

Ailshire, Jennifer A., and Sarah A. Burgard. "Family Relationships and Troubled Sleep among U.S. Adults: Examining the Influences of Contact Frequency and Relationship Quality." *Journal of Health and Social Behavior* 5 (2012): 248–62.

Ajao, Taiwo I., Rosalind P. Oden, Brandi L. Joyner, and Rachel Y. Moon. "Decisions of Black Parents about Infant Bedding and Sleep Surfaces: A Qualitative Study." *Pediatrics* 128 (2011): 494–502.

Allen, Katherine R. "A Conscious and Inclusive Family Studies." *Journal of Marriage and Family* 62 (2000): 4–17.

Amato, Paul R. "Research on Divorce: Continuing Trends and New Developments." *Journal of Marriage and Family* 72 (2010): 650–66.

Anuntaseree, Wanaporn, Ladda Mo-Suwan, Punnee Vasiknanonte, Surachai Kuasirikul, and Chanpen Choprapawan. "Night Waking in Thai Infants at 3 Months of Age: Association between Parental Practices and Infant Sleep." *Sleep Medicine* 9 (2008): 564–71.

Attachment Parenting International. "Infant Sleep Safety." Accessed January 1, 2015, http://www.attachmentparenting.org/infantsleepsafety.

Baddock, Sally A., Barbara C. Galland, Barry J. Taylor, and David P. G. Bolton. "Sleep Arrangements and Behavior of Bed-Sharing Families in the Home Setting." *Pediatrics* 119 (2007): e200–e207.

Ball, Helen. "Parent-Infant Bed-Sharing Behavior: Effects of Feeding Type and Presence of Father." *Human Nature* 17 (2006): 301–18.

Barajas, R. Gabriela, Anne Martin, Jeanne Brooks-Gunn, and Lauren Hale. "Mother-Child Bed-Sharing in Toddlerhood and Cognitive and Behavioral Outcomes." *Pediatrics* 128 (2011): e339–47.

Behm, Ilan, Zubair Kabir, Gregory N. Connolly, and Hillel R. Alpert. "Increasing Prevalence of Smoke-Free Homes and Decreasing Rates of Sudden Infant Death Syndrome in the United States: An Ecological Association Study." *Tobacco Control* 21 (2012): 6–11.

Beijers, Roseriet, J. Marianne Riksen-Walraven, and Carolina de Weerth. "Cortisol Regulation in 12–Month-Old Human Infants: Associations with the Infants' Early History of Breastfeeding and Co-Sleeping." *Stress* 16 (2013): 267–77.

Belluck, Pam. "'Thinking of Ways to Harm Her': New Findings on Timing and Range of Maternal Mental Illness." *New York Times*, June 15, 2014. http://www.nytimes.com/2014/06/16/health/thinking-of-ways-to-harm-her.html.

Bialik, Mayim. *Beyond the Sling*. New York: Simon and Schuster, 2012.

Birditt, Kira S., Karen L. Fingerman, and David M. Almeida. "Age Differences in Exposure and Reactions to Interpersonal Tensions: A Daily Diary Study." *Psychology and Aging* 20 (2005): 330–40.

Boss, Pauline. "Family Stress." In *Handbook of Marriage and the Family*, edited by Marvin B. Sussman and Suzanne K. Steinmetz, 695–723. New York: Plenum, 1987.

Bradbury, Thomas N., Frank D. Fincham, and Steven R. H. Beach. "Research on the Nature and Determinants of Marital Satisfaction: A Decade in Review." *Journal of Marriage and Family* 62 (2000): 964–80.

Breus, Michael J. "Co-Sleeping Increases despite Risks and Recommendations." *Psychology Today*, October 24, 2013. Accessed June 15, 2015, https://www.psychologytoday.com/blog/sleep-newzzz/201310/co-sleeping-increases-despite-risks-and-recommendations.

Bronfenbrenner, Urie. *The Ecology of Human Development: Experiments by Nature and Design*. Cambridge, MA: Harvard University Press, 2009.

Brown, Susan L. "The Effect of Union Type on Psychological Well-Being: Depression among Cohabitors versus Marrieds." *Journal of Health and Social Behavior* 41 (2000): 241–55.

Bureau of Labor Statistics, "Employment Characteristics of Families Summary," Bureau of Labor Statistics, April 22, 2016, accessed October 6, 2016, http://www.bls.gov/news.release/famee.nr0.htm.

Bures, Regina M., Tanya Koropeckyj-Cox, and Michael Loree. "Childlessness, Parenthood, and Depressive Symptoms among Middle-Aged and Older Adults." *Journal of Family Issues* 30 (2009): 670–87.

Cabrera, Natasha J., and Catherine S. Tamis-LeMonda. *Handbook of Father Involvement: Multidisciplinary Perspectives*. London: Routledge, 2013.

Cappuccio, Francesco P., Lanfranco D'Elia, Pasquale Strazzullo, and Michelle A. Miller. "Sleep Duration and All-Cause Mortality: A Systematic Review and Meta-Analysis of Prospective Studies." *Sleep* 33 (2010): 585.

Centers for Disease Control and Prevention. "Insufficient Sleep Is a Public Health Epidemic." Centers for Disease Control and Prevention, September 3, 2015. Accessed January 1, 2016, http://www.cdc.gov/features/dssleep.

Centers for Disease Control and Prevention. "Sudden and Unexpected Infant Death (SUID)." Centers for Disease Control and Prevention. Accessed December 3, 2016, http://www.cdc.gov/sids/pdf/sudden-unexpected-infant-death.pdf.

Centers for Disease Control and Prevention. "Sudden and Unexpected Infant Death and Sudden Infant Death Syndrome." Centers for Disease Control and Prevention, February 8, 2016. Accessed December 3, 2016, http://www.cdc.gov/sids/data.htm.

Cepeda, Marlisse. "Mom Sleeps in Same Bed as Her 9- and 10-Year-Old Sons, Says It's Better for Them." *Woman's Day*, May 19, 2015. Accessed October 7, 2015, http://www.womansday.com/relationships/family-friends/news/a506 46/mom-sleeps-in-the-same-bed-as-her-nine-and-10-year-old-sons.

Cheadle, Jacob E., Paul R. Amato, and Valarie King. "Patterns of Nonresident Father Contact." *Demography* 47 (2010): 205–25.

Cherlin, Andrew J. *The Marriage-Go-Round*. New York: Vintage Books, 2009.

Christopherson, Brian. "Some Buck Trends, Marry before Finishing College." *Ground Zero*, October 6, 2006. Accessed January 4, 2016, http://journalstar.com/entertainment/some-buck-trends-marry-before-finishing-college/article_8c9ad013-c5ad-56a4-9d9b-cf75ac4ea5d9.html.

Chung, Matthew, Rosalind P. Oden, Brandi L. Joyner, Alexandra Sims, and Rachel Y. Moon. "Safe Infant Sleep Recommendations on the Internet: Let's Google It." *Journal of Pediatrics* 161 (2012): 1080–84.

Cohen, Sheldon, and Denise Janicki-Deverts. "Who's Stressed? Distributions of Psychological Stress in the United States in Probability Samples from 1983, 2006, and 2009." *Journal of Applied Social Psychology* 42 (2012): 1320–34.

Coles, Roberta L. "Just Doing What They Gotta Do: Single Black Custodial Fathers Coping with the Stresses and Reaping the Rewards of Parenting." *Journal of Family Issues* 30 (2009): 1311–38.

Colson, Eve R., Marian Willinger, Denis Rybin, Timothy Heeren, Lauren A. Smith, George Lister, and Michael J. Corwin. "Trends and Factors Associated with Infant Bed Sharing, 1993–2010: The National Infant Sleep Position Study." *JAMA Pediatrics* 167 (2013): 1032–37.

Cowan, Carolyn Pape, and Philip A. Cowan. "News You Can Use: Are Babies Bad for Marriage?" Council on Contemporary Families, January 9, 2009. Accessed April 6, 2015, https://contemporaryfamilies.org/news-can-use-babies-bad-marriage.

Cowan, Carolyn Pape, and Philip A. Cowan. *When Partners Become Parents: The Big Life Change for Couples*. Mahwah, NJ: Lawrence Erlbaum Associates Publishers, 2000.

Crawford, Joanne C. "Parenting Practices in the Basque Country: Implications of Infant and Childhood Sleeping Location for Personality Development." *Ethos* 22 (1994): 42–82.

Crnic, Keith A., Catherine Gaze, and Casey Hoffman. "Cumulative Parenting Stress across the Preschool Period: Relations to Maternal Parenting and Child Behavior at Age 5." *Infant and Child Development* 14 (2005): 117–32.

Crnic, Keith A., and Christine Low. "Everyday Stresses and Parenting." In *Handbook of Parenting*, vol. 5, *Practical Issues in Parenting*, edited by Marc H. Bornstein, 243–67. Mahwah, NJ: Lawrence Erlbaum and Associates, 2002.

Dahl, Ronald E., and Mona El-Sheikh. "Considering Sleep in a Family Context: Introduction to the Special Issue." *Journal of Family Psychology* 21 (2007): 1–3.

Daly, Kerry. "Family Theory versus Theory Families Live By." *Journal of Marriage and Family* 65 (2003): 771–84.

DeMaris, Alfred, Annette Mahoney, and Kenneth I. Pargament. "Doing the Scut Work of Infant Care: Does Religiousness Encourage Father Involvement?" *Journal of Marriage and Family* 73 (2011): 354–68.

Dewald, Julia F., Anne M. Meijer, Frans J. Oort, Gerard A. Kerkhof, and Susan M. Bögels. "The Influence of Sleep Quality, Sleep Duration and Sleepiness on School Performance in Children and Adolescents: A Meta-Analytic Review." *Sleep Medicine Reviews* 14 (2010): 179–89.

Dixon, M., N. Booth, and R. Powell. "Sex and Relationships following Childbirth: A First Report from General Practice of 131 Couples." *British Journal of General Practice* 50 (2000): 223–24.

Dollberg, Daphna, Orly Shalev, and Pascale Chen. "'Someone's Been Sleeping in My Bed!' Parental Satisfaction Associated with Solitary and Parent-Child Co-Sleeping in Israeli Families with Young Children." *Early Child Development and Care* 180 (2010): 869–78.

Don, Brian P., and Kristin D. Mickelson. "Relationship Satisfaction Trajectories across the Transition to Parenthood among Low-Risk Parents." *Journal of Marriage and Family* 76 (2014): 677–92.

Doss, Brian D., Galena K. Rhoades, Scott M. Stanley, and Howard J. Markman. "The Effect of the Transition to Parenthood on Relationship Quality: An 8-Year Prospective Study." *Journal of Personality and Social Psychology* 6 (2009): 601.

Duff, Kat. *The Secret Life of Sleep*. New York: Atria Books, 2014.

East, Patricia L., Nina C. Chien, and Jennifer S. Barber. "Adolescents' Pregnancy Intentions, Wantedness, and Regret: Cross-Lagged Relations with Mental Health and Harsh Parenting." *Journal of Marriage and Family* 74 (2012): 167–85.

Ekirch, A. Roger. *At Day's Close: Night in Times Past*. W. W. Norton & Company, 2006.

Fagan, Jay, Randal Day, Michael E. Lamb, and Natasha J. Cabrera. "Should Researchers Conceptualize Differently the Dimensions of Parenting for Fathers and Mothers?" *Journal of Family Theory & Review* 6 (2014): 390–405.

Farooqi, Sadaf, I. J. Perry, and D. G. Beevers. "Ethnic Differences in Sleeping Position and in Risk of Cot Death." *The Lancet* 338 (1991): 1455.

Feiler, Bruce. "Married but Sleeping Alone." *New York Times*, July 25, 2010. Accessed September 3, 2015, http://www.nytimes.com/2010/07/25/fashion/25FamilyMatters.html.

Ferber, Richard. *Solve Your Child's Sleep Problems*. Rev. ed. New York: Simon and Schuster, 2006.

Forbes, John F., David S. Weiss, and Raymond A. Folen. "The Co-Sleeping Habits of Military Children." *Military Medicine* 157 (1992): 196–200.

Fox, Bonnie. *When Couples Become Parents*. Toronto: University of Toronto Press, 2009.

Frosh, Stephen. "Fathers' Ambivalence (Too)." In *Mothering and Ambivalence*, edited by Wendy Hollway and Brid Featherstone, 37–53. New York: Routledge, 1997.

Gay, Caryl L., Kathryn A. Lee, and Shih-Yu Lee. "Sleep Patterns and Fatigue in New Mothers and Fathers." *Biological Research for Nursing* 5 (2004): 311–18.

Glaser, Barney G., and Anselm L. Strauss. *The Discovery of Grounded Theory: Strategies for Qualitative Research*. Piscataway, NJ: Transaction Publishers, 2009.

Glass, George S., and David Tabatsky. *The Overparenting Epidemic*. New York: Skyhorse Publishing, 2014.

Glass, Jennifer, and Philip Levchak. "Red States, Blue States, and Divorce: Understanding the Impact of Conservative Protestantism on Regional Variation in Divorce Rates." *American Journal of Sociology* 119 (2014): 1002–46.

Gottman, John M., and Clifford I. Notarius. "Decade Review: Observing Marital Interaction." *Journal of Marriage and Family* 62 (2000): 927–47.

Gottman, John Mordechai, and Robert Wayne Levenson. "The Timing of Divorce: Predicting When a Couple Will Divorce over a 14-Year Period." *Journal of Marriage and Family* 62 (2000): 737–45.

Grzywacz, Joseph G., Stephanie S. Daniel, Jenna Tucker, Jill Walls, and Esther Leerkes. "Nonstandard Work Schedules and Developmentally Generative Parenting Practices: An Application of Propensity Score Techniques." *Family Relations* 60 (2011): 45–59.

Guttoso, Ashley Nichols. "10 Parenting Debates to Hash Out before Baby." *Parents.* Accessed January 1, 2016, http://www.parents.com/parenting/better-parenting/advice/parenting-debates/#page=7.

Habib, Cherine, Joseph Santoro, Peter Kremer, John Toumbourou, Eva Leslie, and Joanne Williams. "The Importance of Family Management, Closeness with Father and Family Structure in Early Adolescent Alcohol Use." *Addiction* 105 (2010): 1750–58.

Haelle, Tara. "New Guidelines Acknowledge the Reality: Babies Do Sleep in Mom's Bed." *National Public Radio*, October 25, 2016. http://www.npr.org/sections/health-shots/2016/10/25/499290404/new-guidelines-acknowledge-the-reality-babies-do-sleep-in-moms-bed.

Han, Wen-Jui, and Liana E. Fox. "Parental Work Schedules and Children's Cognitive Trajectories." *Journal of Marriage and Family* 73 (2011): 962–80.

Hansson, Malin, and Tone Ahlborg. "Quality of the Intimate and Sexual Relationship in First-Time Parents—A Longitudinal Study." *Sexual & Reproductive HealthCare* 3 (2012): 21–29.

Hauck, Fern R., Cathryn Merrick Moore, Stanislaw M. Herman, Mark Donovan, Mitra Kalelkar, Katherine Kaufer Christoffel, Howard J. Hoffman, and Diane Rowley. "The Contribution of Prone Sleeping Position to the Racial Disparity in Sudden Infant Death Syndrome: The Chicago Infant Mortality Study." *Pediatrics* 110 (2002): 772–80.

Hayes, Marie J., Kelly G. Parker, Bethany Sallinen, and Aditi A. Davare. "Bedsharing, Temperament, and Sleep Disturbance in Early Childhood." *Sleep* 24 (2001): 657–64.

Hayes, Sharon. *The Cultural Contradictions of Motherhood.* New Haven, CT: Yale University Press, 1996.

Henry, James P., and Sheila Wang. "Effects of Early Stress on Adult Affiliative Behavior." *Psychoneuroendocrinology* 23 (1998): 863–75.

Hewlett, Barry S., and Michael E. Lamb. *Hunter-Gatherer Childhoods: Evolutionary, Developmental, and Cultural Perspectives.* Piscataway, NJ: Transaction Publishers, 2005.

Hickson, G. B., and E. W. Clayton. "Parents and Their Doctors." In *Handbook of Parenting*, vol. 5, *Practical Issues in Parenting*, edited by Marc H. Bornstein, 439–62. Mahwah, NJ: Lawrence Erlbaum and Associates, 2002.

Hildingsson, Ingegerd, and Jan Thomas. "Parental Stress in Mothers and Fathers One Year after Birth." *Journal of Reproductive and Infant Psychology* 32 (2014): 41–56.

Hollway, Wendy. "The Maternal Bed: Mothering and Ambivalence." In *Mothering and Ambivalence*, edited by Wendy Hollway and Brid Featherstone, 54–79. New York: Routledge, 1997.

Holmes, Erin Kramer, Takayuki Sasaki, and Nancy L. Hazen. "Smooth versus Rocky Transitions to Parenthood: Family Systems in Developmental Context." *Family Relations* 62 (2013): 824–37.

Huang, Xiao-na, Hui-shan Wang, Li-jin Zhang, and Xi-cheng Liu. "Co-Sleeping and Children's Sleep in China." *Biological Rhythm Research* 41 (2010): 169–81.

Impett, Emily A., Amy Muise, and Diana Peragine. "Sexuality in the Context of Relationships." *APA Handbook of Sexuality and Psychology* 1 (2013): 269–316.

Iwasaki, Yoshi, and Ingrid E. Schneider. "Leisure, Stress, and Coping: An Evolving Area of Inquiry." *Leisure Sciences* 25 (2003): 107–13.

Jackson, Deborah. *Three in a Bed: The Benefits of Sharing Your Bed with Your Baby*. New York: Bloomsbury, 1999.

Jansen, Pauline W., Nathalie S. Saridjan, Albert Hofman, Vincent W. V. Jaddoe, Frank C. Verhulst, and Henning Tiemeier. "Does Disturbed Sleeping Precede Symptoms of Anxiety or Depression in Toddlers? The Generation R Study." *Psychosomatic Medicine* 73 (2011): 242–49.

Jenni, Oskar G., and Bonnie B. O'Connor. "Children's Sleep: An Interplay between Culture and Biology." *Pediatrics* 115 (2005): 204–16.

Jenni, Oskar G., Heidi Zinggeler Fuhrer, Ivo Iglowstein, Luciano Molinari, and Remo H. Largo. "A Longitudinal Study of Bed Sharing and Sleep Problems among Swiss Children in the First 10 Years of Life." *Pediatrics* 115 (2005): 233–40.

Kalil, Ariel, Rachel Dunifon, Danielle Crosby, and Jessica Houston Su. "Work Hours, Schedules, and Insufficient Sleep among Mothers and Their Young Children." *Journal of Marriage and Family* 76 (2014): 891–904.

Kallies, Sarah. "Excuse Me While I Explain What I Meant about Toxic Death Cream," June 22, 2016, http://sarahkallies.com/the-inkwell/2016/6/6/excuse-me-while-i-explain-what-i-meant-about-toxic-death-cream.

Kamp Dush, Claire M., Miles G. Taylor, and Rhiannon A. Kroeger. "Marital Happiness and Psychological Well-Being across the Life Course." *Family Relations* 57 (2008): 211–26.

Kamphuis, Jeanine, Peter Meerlo, Jaap M. Koolhaas, and Marike Lancel. "Poor Sleep as a Potential Causal Factor in Aggression and Violence." *Sleep Medicine* 13 (2012): 327–34.

King, Valarie, Katherine C. Stamps, and Daniel N. Hawkins. "Adolescents with Two Nonresident Biological Parents: Living Arrangements, Parental Involvement, and Well-Being." *Journal of Family Issues* 31 (2009): 3–30.

Komsi, Niina, Katri Räikkönen, Anu-Katriina Pesonen, Kati Heinonen, Pertti Keskivaara, Anna-Liisa Järvenpää, and Timo E. Strandberg. "Continuity of Temperament from Infancy to Middle Childhood." *Infant Behavior and Development* 29 (2006): 494–508.

Koslofsky, Craig. *Evening's Empire: A History of Night in Early Modern Europe*. Cambridge: Cambridge University Press (2011).

Kotila, Letitia E., Sarah J. Schoppe-Sullivan, and Claire M. Kamp Dush. "Time Parenting Activities in Dual-Earner Families at the Transition to Parenthood." *Family Relations* 62 (2013): 795–807.

Kurdek, Lawrence A. "Gender and Marital Satisfaction Early in Marriage: A Growth Curve Approach." *Journal of Marriage and Family* 67 (2005): 68–84.

Latz, Sara, Abraham W. Wolf, and Betsy Lozoff. "Co-Sleeping in Context: Sleep Practices and Problems in Young Children in Japan and the United States." *Archives of Pediatrics & Adolescent Medicine* 153 (1999): 339–46.

Lifshitz, Laura. "Yes, My Daughter Sleeps with Me Sometimes, and No, I Don't Care What You Think." *Huffington Post*, April 20, 2015. Accessed October 7, 2015, http://www.huffingtonpost.com/laura-lifshitz/yes-my-daughter-sleeps-with-me-sometimes-and-no-i-dont-care-what-you-think_b_7089056.html.

Liu, Xianchen, Lianqi Liu, Judith A. Owens, and Debra L. Kaplan. "Sleep Patterns and Sleep Problems among Schoolchildren in the United States and China." *Pediatrics* 115, Supplement 1 (2005): 241–49.

Lozoff, Betsy, George L. Askew, and Abraham W. Wolf. "Co-Sleeping and Early Childhood Sleep Problems: Effects of Ethnicity and Socioeconomic Status." *Journal of Developmental & Behavioral Pediatrics* 17 (1996): 9–15.

Lythcott-Haimes, Julie. *How to Raise an Adult*. New York: Macmillan, 2015.

Maas, Megan K., Brandon T. McDaniel, Mark E. Feinberg, and Damon E. Jones. "Division of Labor and Multiple Domains of Sexual Satisfaction among First-Time Parents." *Journal of Family Issues* (2015). doi:10.1177/0192513X15604343.

MacDorman, Marian F., Donna L. Hoyert, and T. J. Mathews. "Recent Declines in Infant Mortality in the United States, 2005–2011." *NCHS Data Brief* 120 (2013): 1–8.

MacDorman, Marian F., T. J. Mathews, Ashna D. Mohangoo, and Jennifer Zeitlin. "International Comparisons of Infant Mortality and Related Factors: United States and Europe." *National Vital Statistics Reports* 63 (2014). Accessed December 3, 2016, http://www.cdc.gov/nchs/data/nvsr/nvsr63/nvsr63_05.pdf.

MacKenzie, Elmer. "Co-Sleep Blamed in Death of 3 D.M. Babies." *Des Moines Register*, May 22, 2015. Accessed October 6, 2015, http://www.desmoinesregister.com/story/news/crime-and-courts/2015/05/20/babies-die-accidental-smothering-safe-sleep/27651449.

Madansky, Deborah, and Craig Edelbrock. "Co-Sleeping in a Community Sample of 2- and 3-Year-Old Children." *Pediatrics* 86 (1990): 197–203.

Mandara, Jelani, Sheba Y. Rogers, and Richard E. Zinbarg. "The Effects of Family Structure on African American Adolescents' Marijuana Use." *Journal of Marriage and Family* 73 (2011): 557–69.

Margolis, Rachel, and Mikko Myrskylä. "Parental Well-Being Surrounding First Birth as a Determinant of Further Parity Progression." *Demography* 52 (2015): 1147–66.

Maume, David J., Rachel A. Sebastian, and Anthony R. Bardo. "Gender Differences in Sleep Disruption among Retail Food Workers." *American Sociological Review* 74 (2009): 989–1007.

Maume, David J., Rachel A. Sebastian, and Anthony R. Bardo. "Gender, Work-Family Responsibilities, and Sleep." *Gender & Society* 24 (2010): 746–68.

McKenna, James J. *Sleeping with Your Baby*. Washington, DC: Platypus Media (2007).

McKenna, James J. "Sudden Infant Death Syndrome in Cross-Cultural Perspective: Is Infant-Parent Co-Sleeping Protective?" *Annual Review of Anthropology* 25 (1996): 201–16.

McKenna, James J., Helen L. Ball, and Lee T. Gettler. "Mother-Infant Co-Sleeping, Breastfeeding and Sudden Infant Death Syndrome: What Biological Anthropology Has Discovered about Normal Infant Sleep and Pediatric Sleep Medicine." *Yearbook of Physical Anthropology* 50 (2007): 133–61.

Meadows, Robert. "The 'Negotiated Night': An Embodied Conceptual Framework for the Sociological Study of Sleep." *Sociological Review* 53 (2005): 240–54.

Medina, Anna Marie, Crystal L. Lederhos, and Teresa A. Lillis. "Sleep Disruption and Decline in Marital Satisfaction across the Transition to Parenthood." *Families, Systems, & Health* 27 (2009): 153–60.

Meijer, Anne Marie, and Godfried L. H. van den Wittenboer. "Contribution of Infants' Sleep and Crying to Marital Relationship of First-Time Parent Couples in the 1st Year after Childbirth." *Journal of Family Psychology* 21 (2007): 49–57.

Meltzer, Lisa J., Courtney Johnson, Jonathan Crosette, Mark Ramos, and Jodi A. Mindell. "Prevalence of Diagnosed Sleep Disorders in Pediatric Primary Care Practices." *Pediatrics* 125 (2010): e1410–18.

Meltzer, Lisa J., and Jodi A. Mindell. "Relationship between Child Sleep Disturbances and Maternal Sleep, Mood, and Parenting Stress: A Pilot Study." *Journal of Family Psychology* 21 (2007): 67.

Menning, Chadwick L. "'I've Kept It That Way on Purpose': Adolescents' Management of Negative Parental Relationship Traits after Divorce and Separation." *Journal of Contemporary Ethnography* 37 (2008): 586–618.

Messmer, Rosemary, Lynn D. Miller, and Christine M. Yu. "The Relationship between Parent-Infant Bed Sharing and Marital Satisfaction for Mothers of Infants." *Family Relations* 61 (2012): 798–810.

Middlemiss, Wendy, Douglas A. Granger, Wendy A. Goldberg, and Laura Nathans. "Asynchrony of Mother-Infant Hypothalamic-Pituitary-Adrenal Axis Activity following Extinction of Infant Crying Responses Induced during the Transition to Sleep." *Early Human Development* 88 (2012): 227–32.

Milan, Stephanie, Stephanie Snow, and Sophia Belay. "The Context of Preschool Children's Sleep: Racial/Ethnic Differences in Sleep Locations, Routines, and Concerns." *Journal of Family Psychology* 21 (2007): 20–28.

Miles, Matthew B., and Michael A. Huberman. *Qualitative Data Analysis*. 2nd ed. Thousand Oaks, CA: Sage, 1994.

Mindell, Jodi A., Avi Sadeh, Jun Kohyama, and Ti Hwei How. "Parental Behaviors and Sleep Outcomes in Infants and Toddlers: A Cross-Cultural Comparison." *Sleep Medicine* 11 (2010): 393–99.

Mindell, Jodi A., Lorena S. Telofski, Benjamin Wiegand, and Ellen S. Kurtz. "A Nightly Bedtime Routine: Impact on Sleep in Young Children and Maternal Mood." *Sleep* 32 (2009): 599–606.

Morelli, Gilda A., Barbara Rogoff, David Oppenheim, and Denise Goldsmith. "Cultural Variation in Infants' Sleeping Arrangements: Questions of Independence." *Developmental Psychology* 28 (1992): 604–13.

National Sleep Foundation. *2004 Sleep in America Poll*. National Sleep Foundation, March 1, 2004. Accessed February 19, 2015, https://sleepfoundation. org/sites/default/files/FINAL SOF 2004.pdf.

National Sleep Foundation. *2010 Sleep in America Poll*. National Sleep Foundation. Accessed January 1, 2016, http://sleepfoundation.org/sites/default/ files/nsaw/NSF%20Sleep%20in%20%20America%20Poll%20–%20 Summary%20of%20Findings%20.pdf.

National Sleep Foundation. *2012 Bedroom Poll*. National Sleep Foundation, April 1, 2012. Accessed January 1, 2016, http://sleepfoundation.org/sites/ default/files/bedroompoll/NSF_Bedroom_Poll_Report.pdf.

National Sleep Foundation. *2013 International Bedroom Poll*. National Sleep Foundation. Accessed January 1, 2016, http://sleepfoundation.org/sites/ default/files/RPT495a.pdf.

National Sleep Foundation. *2014 Sleep in America Poll: Sleep in the Modern Family*. National Sleep Foundation, March 2014. Accessed January 1, 2016, http://sleepfoundation.org/sites/default/files/2014-NSF-Sleep-in-America-poll-summary-of-findings---FINAL-Updated-3-26-14-.pdf.

Nelson, Margaret. "Reflections on the 25th Anniversary of the Second Shift." American Sociological Association, San Francisco, CA, August 16–19, 2014.

Nolen-Hoeksema, Susan. "Gender Differences in Depression." *Current Directions in Psychological Science* 10 (2001): 173–76.

Nugent, Colleen N., and Lindsey I. Black. "Sleep Duration, Quality of Sleep, and Use of Sleep Medication, by Sex and Family Type, 2013–2014," *NCHS Data Brief* 230 (2016): 1–8.

Okami, Paul, Thomas Weisner, and Richard Olmstead. "Outcome Correlates of Parent-Child Bedsharing: An Eighteen-Year Longitudinal Study." *Journal of Developmental & Behavioral Pediatrics* 23 (2002): 244–53.

Olson, D. H., and D. M. Gorall. "Circumplex Model of Marital and Family Systems." In *Normal Family Processes*, edited by F. Walsh, 514–48 (New York: Guilford, 2003).

Ornelas, India J., Krista M. Perreira, Linda Beeber, and Lauren Maxwell. "Challenges and Strategies to Maintaining Emotional Health: Qualitative Perspectives of Mexican Immigrant Mothers." *Journal of Family Issues* 30 (2009): 1556–75.

Östberg, Monica, and Berit Hagekull. "A Structural Modeling Approach to the Understanding of Parenting Stress." *Journal of Clinical Child Psychology* 29 (2000): 615–25.

Pacey, Susan. "Couples and the First Baby: Responding to New Parents' Sexual and Relationship Problems." *Sexual and Relationship Therapy* 19 (2004): 223–46.

Parade, Stephanie H., A. Nayena Blankson, Esther M. Leerkes, Susan C. Crockenberg, and Richard Faldowski. "Close Relationships Predict Curvilinear Trajectories of Maternal Depressive Symptoms over the Transition to Parenthood." *Family Relations* 63 (2014): 206–18.

Parker, Rozsika. *Torn in Two: The Experience of Maternal Ambivalence.* London: Virago Press Limited, 2005.

Peck, Morgen. "How Co-Sleeping with an Infant Might Make You a Better Dad." *Scientific American Mind* 23 (2013): 8.

Perry-Jenkins, Maureen, JuliAnna Z. Smith, Abbie E. Goldberg, and Jade Logan. "Working-Class Jobs and New Parents' Mental Health." *Journal of Marriage and Family* 73 (2011): 1117–32.

Pert, Karen N. "Baby-Bed-Sharing Trend on the Rise, but Healthcare Providers Can Help Reverse Trend." *Yale News*, September 30, 2013. Accessed January 2, 2016, http://news.yale.edu/2013/09/30/baby-bed-sharing-rise-healthcare-providers-can-help-reverse-trend.

Potter, Carol, and John Carpenter. "Fathers' Involvement in Sure Start: What Do Fathers and Mothers Perceive as the Benefits?" *Practice: Social Work in Action* 22 (2010): 3–15.

Presser, Harriet B. *Working in a 24/7 Economy: Challenges for American Families.* New York: Russell Sage Foundation, 2005.

Pugh, Allison J. *Longing and Belonging: Parents, Children, and Consumer Culture.* Oakland: University of California Press, 2009.

Ramos, Kathleen Dyer, Davin Youngclarke, and Jane E. Anderson. "Parental Perceptions of Sleep Problems among Co-Sleeping and Solitary Sleeping Children." *Infant and Child Development* 16 (2007): 417–31.

Ramsawh, Holly J., Murray B. Stein, Shay-Lee Belik, Frank Jacobi, and Jitender Sareen. "Relationship of Anxiety Disorders, Sleep Quality, and Functional Impairment in a Community Sample." *Journal of Psychiatric Research* 43 (2009): 926–33.

Randall, David K. *Dreamland: Adventures in the Strange Science of Sleep.* New York: W. W. Norton & Company, 2012.

Rankin, Jane L. *Parenting Experts: Their Advice, the Research, and Getting It Right.* Westport, CT: Praeger Publishers, 2005.

Reid, Vanessa, and Mikki Meadows-Oliver. "Postpartum Depression in Adolescent Mothers: An Integrative Review of the Literature." *Journal of Pediatric Health Care* 21 (2007): 289–98.

Robila, Mihaela, and Ambika Krishnakumar. "Economic Pressure and Children's Psychological Functioning." *Journal of Child and Family Studies* 15 (2006): 433–41.

Rosekind, Mark R., Kevin B. Gregory, Melissa M. Mallis, Summer L. Brandt, Brian Seal, and Debra Lerner. "The Cost of Poor Sleep: Workplace Productivity Loss and Associated Costs." *Journal of Occupational and Environmental Medicine* 52 (2010): 91–98.

Rosenberg, Elinor B., and Fady Hajal. "Stepsibling Relationships in Remarried Families." *Social Casework: The Journal of Contemporary Social Work* 66 (1985): 287–92.

Rosenblatt, Paul C. *Two in a Bed: The Social System of Couple Bed Sharing.* Albany: State University of New York Press, 2006.

Rossi, Alice S. "Transition to Parenthood." *Journal of Marriage and the Family* (1968): 26–39.

Sadeh, Avi, Liat Tikotzky, and Anat Scher. "Parenting and Infant Sleep." *Sleep Medicine Reviews* 14 (2010): 89–96.

Saldana, Johnny. *The Coding Manual for Qualitative Researchers.* 2nd ed. Los Angeles: Sage Publications, 2013.

Schachter, Frances Fuchs, Margot L. Fuchs, Polly E. Bijur, and Richard K. Stone. "Co-Sleeping and Sleep Problems in Hispanic-American Urban Young Children." *Pediatrics* 84 (1989): 522–30.

Schalet, Amy T. *Not Under My Roof: Parents, Teens, and the Culture of Sex.* Chicago: University of Chicago Press, 2011.

Schoppe-Sullivan, Sarah J., Sarah C. Mangelsdorf, Geoffrey L. Brown, and Margaret Szewczyk Sokolowski. "Goodness-of-Fit in Family Context: Infant Temperament, Marital Quality, and Early Coparenting Behavior." *Infant Behavior and Development* 30 (2007): 82–96.

Sears, William. *Becoming a Father: How to Nurture and Enjoy Your Family.* Rev. ed. Franklin Park, IL: La Leche League International, 2003.

Shapiro-Mendoza, Carrie K., Eve R. Colson, Marian Willinger, Denis V. Rybin, Lena Camperlengo, and Michael J. Corwin. "Trends in Infant Bedding Use: National Infant Sleep Position Study, 1993–2010." *Pediatrics* (2014): peds-2014.

Siegel, Daniel J. *The Developing Mind.* New York: Guilford Press, 1999.

Smith, Lauren. "This Maternity Bed Totally Changes a New Mom's Hospital Stay." *Good Housekeeping*, December 28, 2015. Accessed December 31, 2015, http://www.goodhousekeeping.com/life/parenting/news/a36148/new-maternity-bed-with-bassinets.

Solomon, Andrew. "The Secret Sadness of Pregnancy with Depression." *New York Times*, May 31, 2015. Accessed August 7, 2015, http://www.nytimes.com/2015/05/31/magazine/the-secret-sadness-of-pregnancy-with-depression.html.

Spiegel, Karine, Esra Tasali, Rachel Leproult, and Eve Van Cauter. "Effects of Poor and Short Sleep on Glucose Metabolism and Obesity Risk." *Nature Reviews: Endocrinology* 5 (2009): 253–61.

Spruyt, Karen, Ivonne Anguh, and Odochi U. Nwabara. "Sleep Behavior of Underrepresented Youth." *Journal of Public Health* 22 (2014): 111–20.

Stanley, Scott M., Galena Kline Rhoades, and Howard J. Markman. "Sliding versus Deciding: Inertia and the Premarital Cohabitation Effect." *Family Relations* 55 (2006): 499–509.

Stein, Martin T., Calvin A. Colarusso, James J. McKenna, and Nancy G. Powers. "Co-Sleeping (Bedsharing) among Infants and Toddlers." *Journal of Developmental & Behavioral Pediatrics* 18 (1997): 408–12.

Strauss, Anselm, and Juliet M. Corbin. *Basics of Qualitative Research.* Vol. 15. Newbury Park, CA: Sage, 1990.

Tahhan, Diana Adis. "Depth and Space in Sleep: Intimacy, Touch and the Body in Japanese Co-Sleeping Rituals." *Body & Society* 14 (2008): 37–56.

Task Force on Sudden Infant Death Syndrome. "SIDS and Other Sleep-Related Infant Deaths: Expansion of Recommendations for a Safe Infant Sleeping Environment." *Pediatrics 128* (2011): e1341–67.

Task Force on Sudden Infant Death Syndrome. "SIDS and Other Sleep-Related Infant Deaths: Updated 2016 Recommendations for a Safe Infant Sleeping Environment." *Pediatrics* 138 (2016): e20162938.

Teachman, Jay. "Military Service, Race, and the Transition to Marriage and Cohabitation." *Journal of Family Issues* 30 (2009): 1433–54.

Teller, Danielle, and Astro Teller. "How American Parenting Is Killing the American Marriage." *Huffington Post*, September 30, 2014. Accessed December 18, 2015, http://www.huffingtonpost.com/2014/10/01/how-american-parenting-is_n_5916064.html.

Thevenin, Tine. *The Family Bed.* New York: Perigee Trade, 2003.

Thomas, Alexander, Stella Chess, and Herbert George Birch. *Temperament and Behavior Disorders in Children.* New York: New York University Press, 1968.

Tollenaar, M. S., Roseriet Beijers, Jarno Jansen, J. M. A. Riksen-Walraven, and Carolina de Weerth. "Solitary Sleeping in Young Infants Is Associated with Heightened Cortisol Reactivity to a Bathing Session but Not to a Vaccination." *Psychoneuroendocrinology* 37 (2012): 167–77.

Trachtenberg, Felicia L., Elisabeth A. Haas, Hannah C. Kinney, Christina Stanley, and Henry F. Krous. "Risk Factor Changes for Sudden Infant Death Syndrome after Initiation of Back-to-Sleep Campaign." *Pediatrics* 129 (2012): 630–38.

Trillingsgaard, Tea, Katherine J. W. Baucom, and Richard E. Heyman. "Predictors of Change in Relationship Satisfaction during the Transition to Parenthood." *Family Relations* 63 (2014): 667–79.

Troxel, Wendy M. "It's More than Sex: Exploring the Dyadic Nature of Sleep and Implications for Health." *Psychosomatic Medicine* 72 (2010): 578–86.

Uhlmann, Eric Luis, and Jeffrey Sanchez-Burks. "The Implicit Legacy of American Protestantism." *Journal of Cross-Cultural Psychology* 45 (2014): 992–1006.

Umberson, Debra, Tetyana Pudrovska, and Corinne Reczek. "Parenthood, Childlessness, and Well-Being: A Life Course Perspective." *Journal of Marriage and Family* 72 (2010): 612–29.

Weigert, Andrew J. *Sociology of Everyday Life*. New York: Longman, 1981.

Weimer, Stephen M., Theresa L. Dise, Patrice B. Evers, Myriam A. Ortiz, Wodajo Welidaregay, and William C. Steinmann. "Prevalence, Predictors, and Attitudes toward Co-Sleeping in an Urban Pediatric Center." *Clinical Pediatrics* 41 (2002): 433–38.

Welles-Nystrom, Barbara. "Co-Sleeping as a Window into Swedish Culture: Considerations of Gender and Health Care." *Scandinavian Journal of Caring Sciences* 19 (2005): 354–60.

Whitbeck, Les B., Ronald L. Simons, Rand D. Conger, K. A. S. Wickrama, Kevin A. Ackley, and Glen H. Elder Jr. "The Effects of Parents' Working Conditions and Family Economic Hardship on Parenting Behaviors and Children's Self-Efficacy." *Social Psychology Quarterly* (1997): 291–303.

Widarsson, Margareta, Gabriella Engström, Andreas Rosenblad, Birgitta Kerstis, Birgitta Edlund, and Pranee Lundberg. "Parental Stress in Early Parenthood among Mothers and Fathers in Sweden." *Scandinavian Journal of Caring Sciences* 27 (2013): 839–47.

Widmer, Eric D., Francesco Giudici, Jean-Marie Le Goff, and Alexandre Pollien. "From Support to Control: A Configurational Perspective on Conjugal Quality." *Journal of Marriage and Family* 71 (2009): 437–48.

Wilcox, W. Bradford, and Jeffrey Dew. "Motherhood and Marriage: A Response." *Journal of Marriage and Family* 73 (2011): 29–32.

Wilson, Katherine R., and Margot R. Prior. "Father Involvement and Child Well-Being." *Journal of Pediatrics and Child Health* 47 (2011): 405–7.

Winnicott, D. W. "Transitional Objects and Transitional Phenomena" *International Journal of Psycho-Analysis* 34 (1953): 89–97.

Wolf, Abraham W., and Betsy Lozoff. "Object Attachment, Thumbsucking, and the Passage to Sleep." *Journal of the American Academy of Child & Adolescent Psychiatry* 28 (1989): 287–92.

Worthman, Carol M., and Ryan A. Brown. "Companionable Sleep: Social Regulation of Sleep and Co-Sleeping in Egyptian Families." *Journal of Family Psychology* 21 (2007): 124–35.

Worthman, Carol M., and Melissa K. Melby. "Toward a Comparative Developmental Ecology of Human Sleep." In *Adolescent Sleep Patterns: Biological, Social, and Psychological Influences*, edited by Mary A. Carskadon, 69–117 (New York: Cambridge University Press, 2002).

Yavorsky, Jill E., Claire M. Kamp Dush, and Sarah J. Schoppe-Sullivan. "The Production of Inequality: The Gender Division of Labor across the Transition to Parenthood." *Journal of Marriage and Family* 77 (2015): 662–79.

INDEX

AAP. *See* American Academy of Pediatrics

ambivalence, 3, 56, 70–74, 78. *See also* co-sleeping: feelings about, perspectives on; guilt; mothers

American Academy of Pediatrics, 1, 2, 5, 11. *See also* Sudden Infant Death Syndrome

attachment, 6, 10, 11, 24, 44, 57, 103, 104, 115

attitudes. *See* co-sleeping: feelings about, perspectives on

Ball, Helen, 33

bedsharing, 1, 4–5, 10, 11, 32–35, 83, 89, 108. *See also* co-sleeping: logistics, location, movement; safety; Sudden Infant Death Syndrome

bedtime routines, 7, 39–40, 47–48, 49, 70

Bialik, Mayim, 10

Boss, Pauline, 21

boys. *See* children; gender

breastfeeding, 4–5, 6, 32–33, 40, 46, 67, 114

CDC. *See* Centers for Disease Control and Prevention

Centers for Disease Control and Prevention, 15

children: gender, 18, 32, 53, 132; infants, 3–5, 11, 32–34, 41, 67, 125; toddlers, 1,

11, 35, 41–42. *See also* participants

cohabitation. *See* family structure

Coles, Roberta, 79

communication, conflict. *See* couples, spouses, partners; communication, conflict. *See also* extended family; friends

co-sleeping: benefits, advantages of, 3, 6–7, 63–67; controversy, debates about, 2, 3, 12, 101, 103, 120, 129; defined, definitions of, 1, 22, 31; disadvantages, negative consequences of, 5–6, 57, 68–77; feelings about, perspectives on, 37, 61–80; historical trends, 18–19; intentional, reactive, 22, 43–46, 57–58; international trends, 16; logistics, location, movement, 29–60; media attention, 1–3, 10, 102, 125, 129, 130; myths about, 1, 42, 59, 126; national trends, 11, 17; safety, 3–5, 34, 75–76; side sleeper, 34, 43, 44; starting, ending, 43–47

couples, spouses, partners: communication, conflict, 58, 86–88, 98; relationship quality, 82–83, 96; sleeping separately, apart, 10, 37–39. *See also* intimacy

crib death. *See* Sudden Infant Death Syndrome

"cry it out". *See* Ferber Method

ABOUT THE AUTHOR

Susan D. Stewart is professor of sociology at Iowa State University. Her scholarship focuses on family dynamics in nontraditional family forms, gender, fertility, and child and adult well-being. Her research has appeared in leading peer-reviewed journals across a wide variety of disciplines, including *Journal of Marriage and Family, Demography, Pediatrics, Family Relations, Journal of Adolescent Health, Journal of Nutrition, Journal of Family Issues, Social Science Research, Population Research and Policy Review*, and *Journal of Family and Economic Issues*. She has conducted research on an array of topics including noncustodial parenting, child and adolescent food insecurity, obesity and nutrition, stepfamily fertility, and women's financial literacy. She has written one book, *Brave New Stepfamilies: Diverse Paths toward Stepfamily Living*, and is the coauthor, with Mary Ann Lamanna and Agnes Riedmann, of *Marriages, Families, and Relationships: Making Choices in a Diverse Society*. Her research has been funded by the National Institute of Child Health and Human Development, the United States Department of Agriculture, the Joint Center for Poverty Research, and the Annie E. Casey Foundation. In addition to her ongoing research on divorce, remarriage, and stepfamilies, Susan Stewart is investigating attachment, child fostering, and adoption.